Future Intelligent Systems and Networks 2019

Future Intelligent Systems and Networks 2019

Editor

Carmen De-Pablos-Heredero

MDPI • Basel • Beijing • Wuhan • Barcelona • Belgrade • Manchester • Tokyo • Cluj • Tianjin

Editor
Carmen De-Pablos-Heredero
Universidad Rey Juan Carlos
Spain

Editorial Office
MDPI
St. Alban-Anlage 66
4052 Basel, Switzerland

This is a reprint of articles from the Special Issue published online in the open access journal *Future Internet* (ISSN 1999-5903) (available at: https://www.mdpi.com/journal/futureinternet/special_issues/Future_2019).

For citation purposes, cite each article independently as indicated on the article page online and as indicated below:

LastName, A.A.; LastName, B.B.; LastName, C.C. Article Title. *Journal Name* **Year**, *Volume Number*, Page Range.

ISBN 978-3-0365-0230-4 (Hbk)
ISBN 978-3-0365-0231-1 (PDF)

Cover image courtesy of Carmen De-Pablos-Heredero.

© 2021 by the authors. Articles in this book are Open Access and distributed under the Creative Commons Attribution (CC BY) license, which allows users to download, copy and build upon published articles, as long as the author and publisher are properly credited, which ensures maximum dissemination and a wider impact of our publications.

The book as a whole is distributed by MDPI under the terms and conditions of the Creative Commons license CC BY-NC-ND.

Contents

About the Editor . . . . **vii**

Carmen De-Pablos-Heredero
Future Intelligent Systems and Networks
Reprinted from: *Future Internet* **2019**, *11*, 140, doi:10.3390/fi11060140 . . . . **1**

Santiago Tejedor, Laura Cervi and Gerard Gordon
Analysis of the Structure and Use of Digital Resources on the Websites of the Main Football Clubs in Europe
Reprinted from: *Future Internet* **2019**, *11*, 104, doi:10.3390/fi11050104 . . . . **3**

César Pérez López, María Jesús Delgado Rodríguez and Sonia de Lucas Santos
Tax Fraud Detection through Neural Networks: An Application Using a Sample of Personal Income Taxpayers
Reprinted from: *Future Internet* **2019**, *11*, 86, doi:10.3390/fi11040086 . . . . **15**

Lingling Zhao, Anping Zhao
Sentiment Analysis Based Requirement Evolution Prediction
Reprinted from: *Future Internet* **2019**, *11*, 52, doi:10.3390/fi11020052 . . . . **29**

Lorenzo J. Torres Hortelano
Audio-Visual Genres and Polymediation in Successful Spanish YouTubers
Reprinted from: *Future Internet* **2019**, *11*, 40, doi:10.3390/fi11020040 . . . . **43**

Diego Corrales-Garay, Eva-María Mora-Valentín and Marta Ortiz-de-Urbina-Criado
Open Data for Open Innovation: An Analysis of Literature Characteristics
Reprinted from: *Future Internet* **2019**, *11*, 77, doi:10.3390/fi11030077 . . . . **65**

About the Editor

Carmen De-Pablos-Heredero is a full time Professor in the Business Administration Area at the Rey Juan Carlos University in Madrid (URJC), Spain. She has been a Visiting Scholar at Norwich University (USA), Queensland University of Technology, QUT (Australia), Durban University of Technology, DUT (South Africa), UTEQ (Ecuador), U. Desarrollo (Chile), and U. Nacional de Tarapacá (Chile). She is the coordinator of the High Performance Research Group OpenInnova. She is director of the Master Degree in Business Organization. Carmen main research specializes in the impact information technology has on organizational systems. She has chaired 35 doctoral dissertations and projects on the impact of information and communication technologies on organizational performance, six of which received international mention. She has presented communications in different international venues and has published more than 150 articles in specialized and indexed journals (JCR and Scopus) and 12 books. Moreover, she has participated in 25 international projects. She has been awarded Campus of Excellence in Energy CEI in 2015, 2017, and 2018. She has also worked as a consultant in IS management at Prima Consulting. She is also the Co-Director of the Master's Degree in Project Management, SAP, Editor or the Academic Review ESIC-Market from July 2016, and WIDS (Women in Data Science, Stanford U.) Ambassador.

Editorial
Future Intelligent Systems and Networks

Carmen De-Pablos-Heredero

Research Groups Open Innova, ESIC UPIs, Strategor and AGR267, Department of Business Organization, Head of the Master Degree in Business Organization and Master of Management of Strategic Logistic Processes, SAP ERP Faculty of Social Sciences, Universidad Rey Juan Carlos, Office 15, Department Building, 28032 Madrid, Spain; carmen.depablos@urjc.es; Tel.: +34-91-488-7545

Received: 5 June 2019; Accepted: 12 June 2019; Published: 25 June 2019

Keywords: open innovation; digital transformation; innovation in communication models, prediction

---

The purpose of this Special Issue is to collect current developments and future directions of Future Intelligent Systems and Networks. This issue is motivated by the progressive implementation of innovative technologies and business models at firms and public organizations. This special issue is a second part of a previous one on the same topic, already published in Future Internet in 2016.

The articles are real experiences that can inspire firms to build more innovative models by properly applying Intelligent Systems and Networks.

The first article, Analysis of the Structure and Use of Digital Resources on the Websites of the Main Football Clubs in Europe, authored by Santiago Tejedor, Laura Cervi, and Gerard Gordon [1], offers a descriptive and comparative analysis of web pages from fifteen best teams in the UEFA ranking. The main objective is analyzing the effectiveness in the management of communication of football clubs. The study concludes, that although the management of communication is effective, none of the analyzed teams have taken full advantage of the possibilities of interaction with the user offered by the digital scenario.

The second article, Tax Fraud Detection through Neural Networks: An Application Using a Sample of Personal Income Taxpayers, authored by César Pérez López, María Jesús Delgado Rodríguez, and Sonia de Lucas Santos [2], is focused on detection of tax fraud concerning personal income tax returns (IRPF, in Spanish) filed in Spain, through the use of Machine Learning advanced predictive tools, by applying Multilayer Perceptron neural network (MLP) models. Results show how the use of neural networks enables taxpayer segmentation and allows the calculation of the probability concerning an individual taxpayer's propensity to attempt to evade taxes. The model presented shows an efficiency rate of 84.3% over other models used to diagnose tax fraud detection.

The third article, Sentiment Analysis Based Requirement Evolution Prediction, authored by Lingling Zhao and Anping Zhao [3], presents a framework that combines a supervised deep learning neural network with an unsupervised hierarchical topic model to analyze user reviews automatically for product feature requirements evolution prediction. The framework allows discovering hierarchical product feature requirements from the hierarchical topic model and identifying their sentiment by the Long Short-term Memory (LSTM) with word embedding. The application of the model to different experiments evidence that effectiveness and feasibility.

The fourth article, Audio-Visual Genres and Polymediation in Successful Spanish YouTubers, authored by Lorenzo J. Torres Hortelano [4], determines the predominant audio-visual genres among the 10 most influential Spanish YouTubers in 2018. Data are extracted from SocialBlade, an independent website, whose main objective is to track YouTube statistics. Results show that polymediation may present an opportunity that has not yet been fully exploited by successful Spanish YouTubers.

The fifth article, Open Data for Open Innovation: An Analysis of Literature Characteristics, authored by Diego Corrales-Garay, Eva-María Mora-Valentín, and Marta Ortiz-de-Urbina-Criado [5], analyzes the journals, conferences, and authors that have published papers about the use of open data for open innovation, the knowledge areas have that have done research on open data for open innovation and the methodological characteristics of articles centered on open data oriented to open innovation. Results show that there is interesting area of research focused in the development of applications of open data for open innovation practices.

These five contributions provide Internet Systems and Networks applications of interest that can become good examples for promote more innovative business models in a variety of industries.

Funding: This research received no external funding.

Conflicts of Interest: The authors declare no conflict of interest.

References

1. Tejedor, S.; Cervi, L.; Gordon, G. Analysis of the Structure and Use of Digital Resources on the Websites of the Main Football Clubs in Europe. *Future Internet* **2019**, *11*, 104. [CrossRef]
2. Pérez López, C.; Delgado Rodríguez, M.J.; De Lucas Santos, S. Tax Fraud Detection through Neural Networks: An Application Using a Sample of Personal Income Taxpayers. *Future Internet* **2019**, *11*, 86. [CrossRef]
3. Zhao, L.; Zhao, A. Sentiment Analysis Based Requirement Evolution Prediction. *Future Internet* **2019**, *11*, 52. [CrossRef]
4. Torres-Hortelano, L. Audio-Visual Genres and Polymediation in Successful Spanish YouTubers. *Future Internet* **2019**, *11*, 40. [CrossRef]
5. Corrales-Garay, D.; Mora-Valentín, E.M.; Ortiz-de-Urbina-Criado, M. Open Data for Open Innovation: An Analysis of Literature Characteristics. *Future Internet* **2019**, *11*, 77. [CrossRef]

© 2019 by the author. Licensee MDPI, Basel, Switzerland. This article is an open access article distributed under the terms and conditions of the Creative Commons Attribution (CC BY) license (http://creativecommons.org/licenses/by/4.0/).

Article

Analysis of the Structure and Use of Digital Resources on the Websites of the Main Football Clubs in Europe

Santiago Tejedor [1],*, Laura Cervi [1] and Gerard Gordon [2]

[1] Department of Journalism and Communication Sciences, Universitat Autonoma de Barcelona, 08193 Bellaterra, Spain; laura.cervi@uab.cat
[2] Department of Communication, Universitat Abat Oliva CEU, 08022 Barcelona, Spain; gerardgg1@gmail.com
* Correspondence: santiago.tejedor@uab.cat; Tel.: +34-93-581-15-45

Received: 24 January 2019; Accepted: 10 April 2019; Published: 29 April 2019

Abstract: Football clubs can be considered global brands, and exactly as any other brand, they need to face the challenge of adapting to digital communications. Nevertheless, communication sciences research in this field is scarce, so the main purpose of this work is to analyze digital communication of the main football clubs in Europe to identify and describe what strategies they follow to make themselves known on the internet and to interact with their users. Specifically, the article studies the characteristics of web pages—considered as the main showcase of a brand/team in the digital environment—of the fifteen best teams in the UEFA ranking to establish what type of structure and what online communication resources they use. Through a descriptive and comparative analysis, the study concludes, among other aspects, that the management of communication is effective, but also warns that none of the analyzed team takes full advantage of the possibilities of interaction with the user offered by the digital scenario.

Keywords: football; clubs; webs; digital communication; marketing; engagement

1. Introduction

Sports have a huge influence in our current society: sport activities occupy an important percentage of people's leisure, becoming both economically and culturally crucial. As the Baron de Coubertin affirmed, "It is a fundamental part of the inheritance of [many]" [1].

Back in 2006, a study of the European Union suggested that, on the one hand, 60% of European citizens actively practice a sport and, on the other, that sport in Europe moves around 407 billion euros, which means 3.7% of EU GDP and employs 15 million people, equivalent to 5.4% of the labor force [2].

With more than 200 million active players, football has become one of the most lucrative leisure industries.

Nowadays, FIFA, the International Federation of Football Association (*Fédération Internationale de Football Association*), the governing body of football federations, has marked the milestone to increase the "participation of more than 60% of the world's population—whether as a player, coach, referee or in any other role—in the world of football" [3] by the 2026 World Cup.

For this reason, many authors have described football as the final stage of the current globalization process [4–7]. If globalization can be defined as the historical process of global integration of the political, economic, social, cultural and technological fields, which has made the world an increasingly interconnected place [5], then football is a clear example of globalization. Accordingly, Boniface points out that football is the "first truly global empire and, unlike others, it has spread throughout the planet in a peaceful way and without the need to impose itself" [5].

Until the early Nineties, football represented a local, national or continental issue, being one of the most protected sectors of the economy, since European teams could only hire a limited number of foreign players (normally three per team), but, in 1995, the "Bosman trial" changed the history of this sport by transforming the richest teams into transnational companies [8]. The free movement of players and the disappearance of the quotas of foreigners, allowed the richest teams of the richest championships (English Premier League, German *Bundesliga*, Spanish *Liga*, Italian *Serie A* and French League) to hire the best players in the world, regardless of their nationality. Proni andand Zaia [9] suggest that, in many rich countries, where market economy dominates the sports scene, football has become a product, transforming some teams into actual global brands with followers all over the world.

This alliance between leisure and business, between sport, show and millionaire profits, cannot be explained without mentioning the massive investment in advertising and mediated sports performance [10]. In other words, the development of technologies, *in primis* television technologies, which allow to live the show of football without having to leave the sofa, have transformed this sport into a mass spectacle. The economic balance of FIFA perfectly illustrates this synergy: the organization, during the year 2015, gained 1,152 million dollars for the organization of tournaments, sales of television broadcast, etc [3].

Summing up, "the transformation of television and the globalization of sport have multiplied mutual economic interests" [11], generating relationships of "symbiosis and parasitism" [12], between actors: sports organizations, commercial organizations and communication groups. The advance in communication technologies, especially digital and satellite television, and subsequently the internet and smartphones [13], have allowed football to acquire a constant and global presence.

In other words, the Digital Revolution and the emergence of Information and Communications Technologies, represent the main challenge for companies and institutions [14], that have to redefine their business model and adapt to these changes [8].

The acronym ICTs, Information and Communications Technologies once used to refer to the convergence of audiovisual and telephone networks, nowadays covers any product that will store, retrieve, manipulate, transmit, or receive information electronically in a digital form [15].

In relation to this, Boyle and Hayes [13] emphasize that sports organizations increasingly try to avoid media control of the messages they broadcast, generating their own communication media, such as television channels and/or internet or mobile marketing applications, which allow them to generate content directly for users.

As we will discuss in the theoretical framework, the study of football communication in the digital environment is quite extended in different disciplines, mostly marketing and sports disciplines [16–18] communication research on this topic, specifically on corporate webpages, is scarce [19]

The study of the corporate portals of the media has been extended to other types of projects and instances [20] of the business, cultural and economic sphere, among others. The works of Ellcelssor [21], Codina et al. [22] have influenced the need to analyze the uses of these web pages. Authors such as Giomelakis and Veglis [23] and Costa-Sánchez and Guarinos Galán [24] have highlighted the importance of assessing a corporate brand, studying its website. In this sense, beyond the digital ecosystem generated by the networks and the set of social platforms, the challenge is to study the role played by the main page or corporate website, conceived as the main information space and as a primary and reference point in the communicative process of an institution, project or organization. Web pages are, thus, considered the embryonic core and the point of reference of the set of digital communication actions that, practically in all cases, lead to this website.

The aim of this study is, therefore, to analyze what strategies main football clubs in Europe use to make themselves known in the cyberspace and interact with their users through their webpages.

The article analyzes the characteristics of web pages—considered as the main showcase of a brand/team in the digital environment—of the fifteen best teams in the ranking of the Union of European Football Associations (UEFA). Based on the above, the article responds to the following research questions with a descriptive scope: "What kind of structure and online communication resources are used by the main football clubs in Europe on their web pages?". In relation to it, and considering the findings of Yoshida, Gordon, Nakazawa and Biscaia [25] about users' engagement, together with Verónica Baena's research [26] on Real Madrid, the following working hypotheses have been considered:

H1. *Soccer clubs in general, tend to choose a very simple web structure that mainly promotes corporate information.*

H2. *The websites design is set up in order to differentiate the club and to emphasize the idiosyncratic elements of each of the clubs.*

H3. *The websites do not fully exploit the possibilities that the digital environment offers them.*

2. Theoretical Framework

2.1. Sports and ICTs

The study of sport is, by definition, multidisciplinary. The interest of the social sciences for sport as a research phenomenon is quite recent; traditional university research took a while to start studying it [1]. Probably, for this reason, sociology—the first discipline that was scientifically interested in sport—both in Anglo–Saxon and Spanish countries [27,28], has long prioritized researches about negative aspects, such as, for example, the association between football and violence. This trend, and the negative connotations given to sport, begun to change progressively in the 70s. In the 90s, football begun to be studied from an economic perspective -for obvious reasons related to the sports industry- and finally as a cultural manifestation and as an agent of social aggregation or reinforcement of identities.

Since then, the interest in sports and precisely football, as an object of study in the field of communication, especially in media studies, has not stopped growing [10]. However, as mentioned above, although there is an extensive bibliography on media and football, especially regarding the image and information that is disseminated through the media, few publications focus on external communication strategies. In addition, most of the works addressing this issue, rarely do so from the digitalization and, specifically, from the analysis of the digital ecosystem perspective [29].

2.2. Marketing and ICTs

Giulianotti [28] states that the goal of sports communication is to transform fans into loyal consumers. The bibliography on football fans is very extensive. In fact, the symbolic nature of football facilitates and enhances the identification with a collective group and the representation of abstract values, such as a brand image. On the one hand, there is a wide sociological tradition that investigates the relationship between soccer teams and followers based on their ability to create identities. Authors, such as Bordieu [30], emphasize that football perfectly captures the notion of imagined community and that imagined communities become more real in the stadium, Hobsbawm [31] demonstrates the ability of this sport to invent traditions that tend to identify the stadium as a mythological place that facilitates the sense of collective identification. Roversi [32] goes so far as to affirm that the fans do not actually support a team but a place, so that the success of their team is synonymous with the success of a place. Nevertheless, these observations do not take into account the aforementioned global dimension of the teams that have followers all over the world as pointed out by Yoshida, Gordon, Nakazawa and Biscaia [25], among others.

In relation to this, taking FC Barcelona as an example, it is likely that for a Catalan follower, *Barça* will be "more than a club" (in the political identity sense), but the same cannot be said of all those fans located in other countries or continents. Probably, the latter will know very little, to say nothing, about this dimension and will not even be very interested. In this sense, Bale [33] recognizes that football represents a powerful mean of collective identification with a place, but also serves to project a place to people who otherwise would not have known it. Therefore, other authors have devoted themselves to the study of the follower of this sport as a consumer. Moragas [34], for example, highlights the difference between the consumer of sport and the consumer of other products, emphasizing that the followers of sport clubs develop a blind loyalty to their team that helps them not to leave it aside even when the results are not positive. In the words of Roberts [35], they generate a "loyalty beyond reason".

By contrast, Ferran Soriano [36], former economic vice president of FC Barcelona, openly criticizes this paradigm stating that the team is the product and if there is no product [the team does not meet the expectations of the fans] marketing or any other actions become completely useless.

According to Yoshida, Gordon, Nakazawa and Biscaia [25], sport fans generate unique behavioral responses.

Based on this, it is quite evident that a football clubs shares with any other company the challenge of adapting their communication to the digital environment. This becomes evident observing Table 1, which shows the increase in sport advertising investment in Europe.

Table 1. Advertising investments.

Media	2013	2014	2015	Increase	2016
TV	1.703,4	1.890,4	2.011,3	5.5%	2.121,6
Digital	960,1	1.065,6	1288,9	21.5%	1.565,6
Newspapers	662,9	656,3	658,9	−6.3%	617,4
Radio	403,6	420,2	454,4	0.8%	458,0
Posters	282,0	314,7	327,4	−2.0%	321,0
Magazines	254,9	254,2	255,2	−1.2%	252,2
Sunday Newspapers	38,7	37,7	37,8	−10.6%	33,8
Cinema	20,2	16,2	22,0	2.7%	22,6
Total	4.324,8	4.655,3	5.055,9	8.6%	5.392,5

Source: *La Vanguardia*, adapted by the authors.

Both communication sciences, and social sciences, such as sociology, and economic disciplines, especially marketing, have understood that the paradigm of communication has changed with the appearance of new technologies, which allow users to be connected at all times [29] to get a potentially infinite amount of information and interactions. Jenkins (2015) states that Web 2.0 has become a kind of cultural dynamic that encompasses any digital business with the aim of capturing and exploiting the participatory culture [37]. Costa and Piñeiro [38] emphasize that the impact of interactivity in narrative transforms the traditional storytelling techniques in favor of a horizontal, collaborative and social dialogic logic.

In this context, marketing has invented a new word that summarizes all these concepts: prosumer. The word prosumer is an acronym that comes from the merger of two words: "producer" and "consumer". The concept, anticipated by McLuhan and Nevitt [39], and disseminated by Levine, Locke, Searls and Weinberger [40], refers to the fact that electronic technology allows the consumer to simultaneously assume the roles of producer and consumer of content. This new scenario, somehow forces organizations to opt for the resource of conversation, understanding cyberspace as a context endowed with a great capacity to multiply intellectual capital. In this way, it is key to establish a new communicative relationship between sender and receiver, since the user ceases to be a passive testimony of the information to be an actor and participate in this communicative act [41].

In response to this trend, digital corporate communication emerges, which encompasses the set of actions necessary to advertise the activity of the organization on the Web and, in particular, to satisfy the demand of what the different publics want [42]. Its main objective is to get more users on the website or, in other word, generate loyalty and engagement [43].

The concept of engagement has been recently defined as a set of behavioral manifestations of the client towards the company (commitment and loyalty, mainly) above the mere purchase action that occurs as a result of individual motivations. These behaviors can be defined non-transactional and are especially valuable for companies because, although they do not generate immediate income, they improve their image and influence on long-term consumers. In other words, everything it is based on getting the largest possible number of users to share the published content, thus creating a network of influences based on the amount of "likes", visualizations or the specific metric of the platform, depending on the type of material and the platform used.

Studies like those of Ioakimidis [15], Araujo et al. [17], Baena [18] have investigated the impact of dialogical platforms, digital marketing or mobile telephony in the sports arena. However, the study of corporative website as the main unit of information, communication and interaction, has been given scarce importance and prominence.

Nevertheless, UEFA's Club Licensing Benchmarking Report of 2016, underlines that clubs that generate the most visitors to their websites tend to have a broad reach that encompasses their domestic market and other global markets [44].

Accordingly, our research will focus on web pages, understood as the main information space and the primary and reference point in the communicative process of an institution [22].

3. Method

Based on the above, our research analyzes, using descriptive and comparative methods, the digital ecosystem of the fifteen major football clubs in Europe, focusing on the detailed study of their web pages. Clubs have been selected according to UEFA's (Union of European Football Associations) ranking, listing the best clubs in Europe for their performance over the last five seasons, acknowledging that the best performing clubs may not be the clubs with the highest amount of followers/traffic.

The selected teams, as shown by Table 2, are: Real Madrid CF (Spain), FC Bayern München (Germany), FC Barcelona (Spain), Club Atlético de Madrid (Spain), Juventus (Italy), Paris Saint-Germain (Paris), Borussia Dortmund (Germany), Sevilla CF (Spain), SL Benfica (Portugal), Chelsea FC (England), Arsenal FC (England), Manchester City FC (England), FC Porto (Portugal) and Manchester United FC (England).

Table 2. Club sample.

Real Madrid CF (Spain)	FC Bayern München (Germany)	FC Barcelona (Spain)	Club Atlético de Madrid (Spain)	Juventus (Italy)
Paris Saint-Germain (France)	Borussia Dortmund (Germany)	Sevilla FC (Spain)	SL Benfica (Portugal)	Chelsea FC (UK)
Arsenal FC (UK)	Manchester City F.C. (UK)	FC Porto (Portugal)	FC Schalke 04 (Germany)	Manchester United FC (UK)

Source: elaborated by the authors.

Analysis of the Webpages

In order to classify and describe the different components of the main digital platform (website) of each of the analyzed club, we have created a four level framework, taking into account home page, header and bottom frame, and the typology and design of the contents published on the website.

Our framework, displayed in Table 3, is adapted from the proposal of Rodriguez-Martinez, Codina, and Pedraza-Jiménez [45], based on Landow's [46] classic model of hypertext analysis.

Table 3. Level of the analysis.

Level 0: General information	This level assess the basic information of the club. Specifically, the existence of a web page, the number of languages of the contents offered and the type of domain used.
Level 1: Superior frame or header	This level of analysis collects information on the header of the page focusing on whether the club has other sports sections, if there is a search option on the menu, if it offers the chance to register to have exclusive content and if there is a virtual store.
Level 2: Type and content design	This level analyzes in detail, from a descriptive approach, the information of the articles, such as elements of title, type and presence of multimedia content, use and type of hyperlinks. In addition, the possibility of interaction of Internet users is also assessed, as well as other information relevant to the user's browsing experience.
Level 3: Inferior Frame	This level analyzes the bottom frame of the page: the sponsors of the club, the access to social networks, the type of physical design of the template and the structure of the navigation menu.

Source: elaborated by the authors.

4. Results

Although nowadays the most important source of communication are social networks, the study has established that most of the messages broadcasted by clubs originate on their official website. Specifically, the study establishes that the clubs mostly use the contents of their website to feed the contents of all the platforms that make up their respective digital ecosystems.

In this section, we will present the main results, classified by different categories or thematic areas:

Plurality of languages. Clubs are not only known in their country of origin, since as global brands they have followers around the world. Therefore, they face the need to reach a greater number of countries. The translation of the content into several languages is thus fundamental, and there are differences in the number of languages used by the websites. Specifically, as shown by Figure 1, clubs offer an average of six languages: only four teams do not reach this number of translations (Oporto, Arsenal, Benfica and Atlético de Madrid), an aspect that affects its territorial scope compared to the rest.

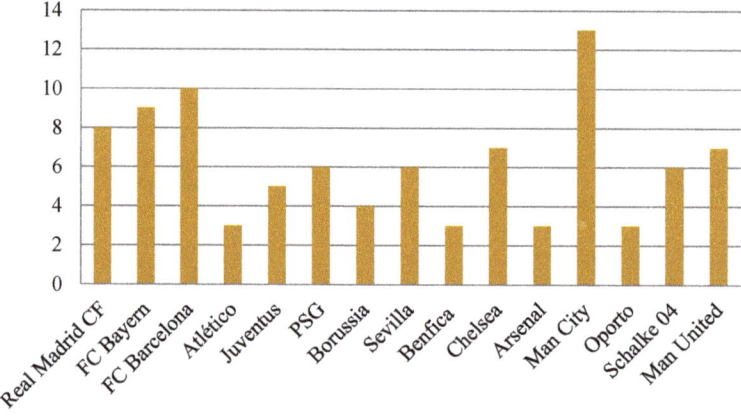

Figure 1. Number of languages available in the webpages. **Source**: Elaborated by the authors.

Distribution of the header. Table 4 shows that there is a predominance of the use of the horizontal bar with the section keypads with several options to navigate. The registration and login options are located in the upper right, next to the search button. These last two options are present in 80% of the clubs analyzed and only one of them (FC Oporto) does not have a store option on the menu. It is also common to see a clear distinction between the navigation menu and the menu for selling club products (or merchandising line).

Table 4. Distribution of the header.

	Sections	Search Engine	Registration	Store	Social Networks	Pattern	E-Commerce
Real Madrid	Yes	Yes	Yes	Yes	No	No	Yes
FC Bayern	No	Yes	Yes	Yes	No	No	Yes
FC Barcelona	Yes	Yes	Yes	Yes	Yes	No	Yes
Atlético	Female	Yes	Yes	Yes	Yes	No	No
Juventus	No	Yes	Yes	Yes	No	No	No
PSG	Female	No	Yes	Yes	No	No	No
Borussia	No	Yes	Yes	Yes	Yes	Yes	No
Sevilla	Female	Yes	No	Yes	No	No	No
Benfica	Yes	Yes	Yes	Yes	In the menu	No	No
Chelsea	Female	Yes	Yes	Yes	No	No	No
Arsenal	Female	Yes	Yes	Yes	No	No	No
Man City	No	No	Yes	Yes	No	No	No
Oporto	Yes	No	No	No	No	No	No
Schalke 04	Yes	Yes	No	Yes	Yes	No	No
Man United	no	Yes	Yes	Yes	Yes	no	no

Source: Elaborated by the authors.

Moreover, only five teams, Atletico, PSG, Sevilla, Chelsea and Arsenal dedicate a space to the so-called "female section", that is to say the female team.

Extension of the domain. Figure 2 shows that 66.7% of the clubs opt for the .com domain to reach a more global community, because it is a generic superior domain, while the rest use the territorial domain of their country of origin. In this group, we must highlight the case of *Fútbol Club Barcelona*, whose first option of viewing is under the .cat domain, typical of Catalonia, although it also has others depending on the user's location.

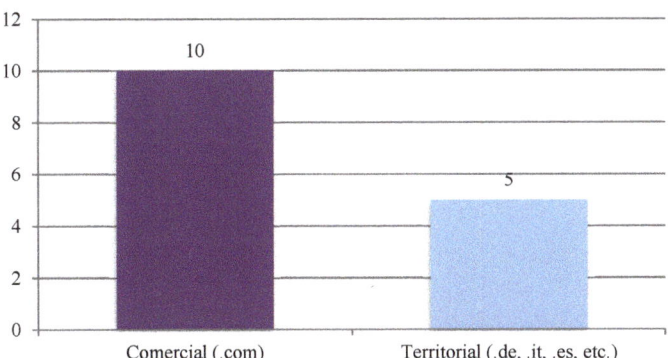

Figure 2. Domain extension. **Source**: elaborated by the authors.

Content design. The distribution of content is based on a structured pattern with news highlighted with bigger fonts. In addition, it is important to mention that 40% of the teams have advertising on their website, a fact that can impoverish user experience and increase the rate of abandonment of the platform.

Table 5 shows the content design. The category "Title" takes into consideration whether the page has only the Tile (1), a Pre-Tile (2) or also a Subtitle (3).

Table 5. Content design and type.

	Titles	Images	Videos	Figures	Links	Context	Enlargement	Concept
Real Madrid CF	1, 3	Yes	Yes	No	Yes	No	Yes	Yes
FC Bayern	1,2,3	Yes	Yes	No	No	No	No	No
FC Barcelona	1	Yes	Yes	No	Yes	Yes	Yes	Yes
Atlético	1, 2,3	Yes	Yes	No	Yes	Yes	Yes	Yes
Juventus	1	Yes	Yes	No	Yes	No	Yes	No
PSG	1	Yes	Yes	No	Yes	No	Yes	No
Borussia	1	Yes	Yes	No	Yes	No	Yes	No
Sevilla	1	Yes	Yes	No	Yes	No	Yes	No
Benfica	1, 3	Yes	Yes	No	No	No	No	No
Chelsea	1, 3	Yes	Yes	No	Yes	No	No	Yes
Arsenal	1, 3	Yes	Yes	No	Yes	Yes	Yes	Yes
Manchester City	1	Yes	Yes	No	Yes	Yes	Yes	Yes
Oporto	1	Yes	Yes	No	No	No	No	No
Schalke 04	1, 2,3	Yes	Yes	No	Yes	No	No	Yes
Manchester United	1	Yes	Yes	No	Yes	No	Yes	No

Source: elaborated by the authors.

Use of multimedia and interactive resources. The study concludes that all the clubs analyzed offer a great variety of images and videos, as well as links to other news sources in their web pages. However, as shown by Table 6, none of the clubs allows users to actively interact (through comments or other dialogical channels).

Table 6. Use of multimedia and interactive resources.

	Advertising	Audio	List	Interactivity	Social Networks	Newsletter
Real Madrid CF	Yes	No	No	No	Yes	Yes
FC Bayern	No	No	No	No	Yes	Yes
FC Barcelona	Yes	No	No	Indirect	Yes	Yes
Atlético	Yes	No	Yes	No	Yes	Yes
Juventus	Yes	No	Yes	No	Yes	Yes
PSG	Yes	No	Yes	No	Yes	Yes
Borussia	Yes	No	Yes	No	Yes	Yes
Sevilla	Yes	No	Yes	No	Yes	Not official
Benfica	Yes	No	Yes	No	Yes	Not official
Chelsea	No	No	No	No	Yes	Yes
Arsenal	No	No	No	No	Yes	Yes
Man City	No	No	No	No	Yes	No
Oporto	No	No	No	No	Yes	Yes
Schalke 04	No	No	No	No	Yes	Yes
Manchester United	Yes	No	No	No	Yes	Yes

Source: elaborated by the authors.

Link to social networks. Table 7 displays how most of the clubs redirect the content to generate a significant influx of visitors to the networks and thus obtain a greater number of followers. In this regard, it is worth mentioning that all clubs have a link to their complementary platforms on their website, but the position of these hyperlinks in the lower part of the page is preferable. Of the selected sample, 80% of the teams follow this premise, although there is 40% of it that includes it in the upper frame (so in some cases we can observe a repetition of links in both locations).

Table 7. Design of the bottom frame.

	Sponsors	Social Networks	Pattern	Menu
Real Madrid CF	Yes	Yes	No	Yes
FC Bayern	Yes	Yes	No	Yes
FC Barcelona	Yes	Yes	Yes	No
Atlético	Yes	Yes	No	No
Juventus	Yes	Yes	No	No
PSG	Yes	Yes	No	No
Borussia	Yes	Yes	No	No
Sevilla	Yes	Yes	No	Yes
Benfica	Yes	Yes	No	No
Chelsea	Yes	Yes	Yes	No
Arsenal	No	No	No	No
Manchester City	Yes	Yes	Yes	No
Oporto	Yes	No	No	Yes
Schalke 04	Yes	Yes	No	No
Manchester United	No	no	No	No

Source: elaborated by the authors.

5. Conclusions

In this section, we will comment on the formulated hypothesis.

H4. *Soccer clubs generally choose a very simple web structure providing mainly corporate information.*

The development of the contextual study on digital communication and presence on the Internet, together with the analysis carried out by the aforementioned clubs, makes it possible to determine that the management of communication is effective, but it can be improved in different way. In all cases, interaction should be emphasized, an aspect that has a decisive value to achieve a more important navigation at the user level. The most remarkable aspect of the analysis is that none of the teams offers elements of interaction, such as the option to comment on news or a "like" button, among other options. There are, however, elements of indirect interaction, as in the case of Arsenal, which collects tweets from fans in a sector of its website. Even so, this is very limited and web pages do not stop being one-way information portals, an aspect that does not allow enhancing the collaborative and participative essence of the cyberspace. Web pages satisfactorily collect the interests of the club in the form of news and general content for the fans. Some teams, such as Oporto FC, Schalke 04 or Benfica, present a web page of a shorter and simpler nature than that of the other teams. This aspect allows us to affirm that there is a correlation between the difference in importance and role of clubs and their digital communication, despite the fact that one of them is the club with the highest amount of members in Europe. Finally, and in line with what mentioned above, we underline the need for clubs to exploit the interaction with the user at a general level.

H5. *The design of the websites denotes an effort to differentiate themselves and emphasize the idiosyncratic elements of clubs.*

There are a number of common aspects that determine a clear pattern in most web pages, such as the predominance of club colors (the Real Madrid page is white, Barcelona's page is *blaugrana*, etc.), but there are those that break with this dynamic to be more original and distribute the information in another way. In Borussia Dortmund's web, for example, the menu bar of is in diagonal instead of the traditional horizontal position. It also has a clearly differentiated distribution of its cover contents, organized in two columns, while the rest of the teams dislay their content horizontally. Another relevant case is that of the two Manchester teams. First, the City distributes its content in in two columns, but unlike Borussia, these are independent. This aspect allows the user to surf through the left column as the main web page and, subsequently, through the column on the right where recent news, tweets and other data presented in a more dynamic way. Secondly, United presents a more disruptive system, since it leaves the traditional horizontal bar to place it on the left side of the page, in vertical position.

H6. *Soccer clubs do not fully exploit the possibilities that the digital environment offers them.*

According to our analysis, clubs opt for a set of valid multimedia strategies, such as the inclusion of videos, pictures or links to social networks that stimulate interaction and navigation through their website. Even so, cyberspace allows the inclusion of other types of resources beyond the audiovisual ones. The interactive and participative idiosyncrasy of the Network is not fully implemented.

In conclusion, we consider that, in order to increase engagement, clubs should implement a system of interaction, such as transmedia narrative and stories, since the exploitation of the multimedia and transmedia component is, for the moment, very limited.

6. Discussion

The study delves into the need to expand academic work around the convergence of areas of study such as communication, social networks and sports. Both 2.0 and 3.0 environment offer many possibilities yet to be discovered. At the communicative level, it would be interesting to foster the research on aspects such as transmedia narrative or storytelling, which could enrich the digital content and improve the user experience, as well as the interaction between follower and club through collaborative platforms and digital communication tools offered by cyberspace. In this same line of discussion, enhancing interaction would improve clubs' transparency and their (virtual) proximity with followers.

This aspect raises the need to abandon the traditional communication model and adapt to the current new paradigm, exploiting more innovative multimedia resources.

Author Contributions: Conceptualization, L.G. and S.T.; methodology, G.G.; software, G.G.; validation, S.T. and L.G.; formal analysis, G.G.; investigation, G.G.; data curation, S.T.; writing—original draft preparation, L.G.; writing—review and editing, L.G.; visualization, S.T.

Funding: This research received no external funding.

Conflicts of Interest: The authors declare no conflicts of interest.

References

1. Cervi, L. *Identitat i Fútbol: El Clàssic Espanyol vist des d'Europa*; Fundació Esport i Ciutadania, Pagès: Lleida, Spain, 2013.
2. European Commission. *White Paper on Sport*; Comissió Europea: Brusselles, Belgium, 2007.
3. FIFA. Informe de Finanzas y Gobernanza 2015, des de. 2016. Available online: http://resources.fifa.com/mm/document/affederation/administration/02/77/08/71/gb15_fifa_web_es_spanish.pdf (accessed on 22 December 2019).
4. Sebreli, J.J. *La Era del Fútbol*; Editorial Debolsillo: Buenos Aires, Argentina, 1998; ISBN 9789875660496. Available online: http://books.google.com.ar/books?id=RH7ewye6IcEC (accessed on 4 January 2019).
5. Boniface, P. *La Terre est Ronde Comme un Ballon. Géopolitique du Football*; Seuil: Paris, France, 2002.
6. Poli, R. L'Europe à Travers le Prisme du Football. Nouvelles Frontières Circulatoires et Redéfinition de la Nation. Available online: https://journals.openedition.org/cybergeo/2802 (accessed on 7 January 2019).
7. Milanovic, B. Globalization and goals: Does soccer show the way? *Int. Econ.* **2005**, *12*, 829–850. [CrossRef]
8. Lule, J. *Globalization and Media: Global Village of Babel*; Rowman & Littlefield: Lanham, MD, USA, 2017.
9. Proni, M.W.; Zaia, F.H. Gestão empresarial do futebol num mundo globalizado. In *Futebol e Globalização*; Ribeiro, L., Ed.; Fontoura: Jundiaí, Brazil, 2007.

10. Meneses, G.A.; Avalos González, J.M. La investigación del futbol y sus nexos con los estudios de comunicación: Aproximaciones y ejemplos. *Comunicación y Sociedad* **2013**, *20*, 33–64.
11. De Sousa, A.L.N.; Cervi, L. Video activism in the Brazilian protests: genres, narratives and political participation. *Northern Lights* **2017**, *15*, 69–88. [CrossRef]
12. Solberg, H.Y.; Helland, K. Sports Broadcasting. *Nord. Rev.* **2011**, *32*, 17–33. [CrossRef]
13. Boyle, R.; Haynes, R. *Sport, the Media and Strategic Communications Management*; Routledge: London, UK, 2011.
14. Wu, J.; Guo, S.; Huang, H.; Liu, W.; Xiang, Y. Information and Communications Technologies for Sustainable Development Goals: State-of-the-Art, Needs and Perspectives. *IEEE Commun. Surv. Tutor.* **2018**, *20*, 2389–2406. [CrossRef]
15. Zuppo Colrain, M. Defining ICT in a Boundaryless World: The Development of a Working Hierarchy. *Int. J. Manag. Inf. Technol.* **2012**, *4*, 13. [CrossRef]
16. Ioakimidis, M. Online marketing of professional sports clubs: Engaging fans on a new playing field. *Int. J. Sports Mark. Spons.* **2010**, *11*, 2–13. [CrossRef]
17. Araujo, N.; De Carlos, P.; Fraiz, J.A. Top European football clubs and social networks: A true 2.0 relationship? *Sport Bus. Manag. Int. J.* **2014**, *4*, 250–264. [CrossRef]
18. Baena, V. Getting Brand Commitment through Internet and Mobile Sports Marketing. In *Handbook of Research on Digital Marketing Innovations in Social Entrepreneurship and Solidarity Economics*; IGI Global: Hershey, PA, USA, 2014; pp. 203–218.
19. Nisar, T.M.; Prabhakar, G.; Patil, P.P. Patil, Sports clubs' use of social media to increase spectator interest. *Int. J. Inf. Manag.* **2018**, *43*, 188–195. [CrossRef]
20. Lopezosa, C.; Codina, L.; Rovira, C. *Visibilidad Web de Portales de Televisión y Radio en España: ¿qué Medios Llevan a Cabo un Mejor Posicionamiento en Buscadores? Serie DigiDoc-EPI, n*; Ediciones Profesionales de la Información SL.: Barcelona, Spain, 2019; ISBN 978-84-09-07716-8.
21. Ellcessor, E. Captions On, Off, on TV, Online: Accessibility and Search Engine Optimization in Online Closed Captioning. *Telev. New Media* **2012**, *13*, 329–352. [CrossRef]
22. Codina, L.; Iglesias-García, M.; Pedraza, R.; García-Carretero, L. *Visibilidad y Posicionamiento Web de Informaciones Periodísticas: El Framework SEO-RCP*; Serie Editorial DigiDoc-UPF: Barcelona, Spain, 2016; Available online: http://repositori.upf.edu/handle/10230/26040 (accessed on 22 February 2019).
23. Giomelakis, D.; Veglis, A. Investigating Search Engine Optimization Factors in Media Websites, The case of Greece. *Digit. J.* **2016**, *4*, 379–400. [CrossRef]
24. Costa-Sánchez, C.; Guarinos, V. Gestión de marca corporativa online de los canales públicos de televisión en Europa. Propuesta de indicadores para su medición. *Revista Latina de Comunicación Social* **2018**, *73*, 895–910.
25. Yoshida, M.; Gordon, B.; Nakazawa, M.; Biscaia, R. Conceptualization and Measurement of Fan Engagement: Empirical Evidence from a Professional Sport Context. *J. Manag.* **2014**, *28*, 399–417. [CrossRef]
26. Baena, V. Analyzing online and mobile marketing strategies as brand love drivers in sports teams. Findings from Real Madrid. *Int. J. Sports Mark. Spons.* **2016**, *17*, 202–218. [CrossRef]
27. Dunning, E. *Sport et Civilisation. La Violence Maîtrisée*; Fayard: Paris, France, 1994.
28. Giulianotti, R. Fanáticos, seguidores, fas e flaneurs: Uma taxonomia do identidades do torcedor no futebol. *Recorde Revista de História do Esporte* **2012**, *5*, 123–190.
29. Akbal, E.; Güneş, F.; Akbal, A. Digital Forensic Analyses of Web Browser Records. *J. Softw.* **2016**, *11*, 631–637. [CrossRef]
30. Bordieu, P. Deporte y Clase Social. In *Materiales de Sociología del Deporte*; La Piqueta: Madrid, Spain, 1993.
31. Hobsbawm, E.J. *Naciones y Nacionalismo Desde Crítica*; Grijaldo Mondadori: Barcelona, Spain, 1992.
32. Roversi, A. *Calcio e Violenza in Europa*; Il Mulino: Bologna, Italy, 1990.
33. Bale, J. Playing at home: British football and a sense of place. In *British Football and Social Change: Getting into Europe*; Williams, J., Wagg, S., Eds.; Leicester University Press: Leicester, UK, 1991.
34. Moragas, M. *El Impacto de Internet en Los Medios de Comunicación y la Industria del Deporte*; Centre d'Estudis Olímpics, Bellaterra Universitat Autònoma de Barcelona: Barcelona, Spain, 2003.

35. Roberts, K. Lovemarks: The Future Beyond Brands. Power House Books: New York, NY, USA, 2005. Available online: https://s3.amazonaws.com/academia.edu.documents/44012240/LoveMarks.pdf?AWSAccessKeyId=AKIAIWOWYYGZ2Y53UL3A&Expires=1556514093&Signature=tcIoir96Ef8zeCnSTvQmC28nVlc%3D&response-content-disposition=inline%3B%20filename%3DTHE_FUTURE_BEYOND_BRANDS.pdf (accessed on 29 April 2019).
36. Soriano, F. *La Pilota No Entra Per Atzar*; Ara llibres: Badalona, Italy, 2009.
37. Kiruthika, J.; Greenhill, D.; Francik, J.; Khaddaj, S. User Experience Design in Web Applications. In Proceedings of the 2016 IEEE Intl Conference on Computational Science and Engineering (CSE) and IEEE Intl Conference on Embedded and Ubiquitous Computing (EUC) and 15th Intl Symposium on Distributed Computing and Applications for Business Engineering (DCABES), Paris, France, 24–26 August 2016; pp. 642–646.
38. Costa, C.; Piñeiro, T. *Estrategias de Comunicación Multimedia*; Editorial UOC: Barcelona, Spain, 2013.
39. McLuhan, M.; Nevitt, B. *Take Today: The Executive as Dropout*; Harcourt Brace Jovanovich: New York, NY, USA, 1972.
40. Levine, R.; Locke, C.; Searls, D.; Weinberger, D. The Cluetrain Manifesto. 1999. Available online: http://www.cluetrain.com (accessed on 21 January 2012).
41. Tejedor, S. *La Enseñanza del Ciberperiodismo en Las Licenciaturas de Periodismo de España*; Universitat Autònoma de Barcelona: Barcelona, Spain, 2006.
42. Rincón Quintero, Y.R. Vinculación de relaciones públicas, comunicación corporativa, y logística en la organización. *Revista Encuentros Universidad Autónoma del Caribe* **2014**, *12*, 47–59.
43. Chiou, W.-C.; Lin, C.-C.; Perng, C. A strategic framework for website evaluation based on a review of the literature from 1995–2006. *Inf. Manag.* **2010**, *47*, 282–290. [CrossRef]
44. UEFA. Club Licensing Benchmarking Report Financial Year. 2016. Available online: https://www.uefa.com/MultimediaFiles/Download/OfficialDocument/uefaorg/Clublicensing/02/53/00/22/2530022_DOWNLOAD.pdf (accessed on 7 October 2018).
45. Rodríguez-Martínez, R.; Codina, L.; Pedraza-Jiménez, R. Rafael Indicadores para la evaluación de la calidad en cibermedios: Análisis de la interacción y de la adopción de la Web 2. *Revista Española de Documentación Científica* **2012**, *35*, 61–93. [CrossRef]
46. George, P. *Landow, Hypertext 3.0: Critical Theory and New Media in an Era of Globalization*; Johns Hopkins University Press: Baltimore, MD, USA, 2006.

© 2019 by the authors. Licensee MDPI, Basel, Switzerland. This article is an open access article distributed under the terms and conditions of the Creative Commons Attribution (CC BY) license (http://creativecommons.org/licenses/by/4.0/).

Article

Tax Fraud Detection through Neural Networks: An Application Using a Sample of Personal Income Taxpayers

César Pérez López [1], María Jesús Delgado Rodríguez [2,*] and Sonia de Lucas Santos [3]

[1] Instituto de Estudios Fiscales, Universidad Rey Juan Carlos, 28670 Madrid, Spain; cesar.perez@urjc.es or cesar.perez@ief.minhafp.es
[2] Economía de la Empresa (ADO), Economía Aplicada II y Fundamentos Análisis Económico, Universidad Rey Juan Carlos, 28670 Madrid, Spain
[3] Facultad de Ciencias Económicas y Empresariales, Universidad Autónoma de Madrid, Ciudad Universitaria de Cantoblanco, 28049 Madrid, Spain; sonia.delucas@uam.es
* Correspondence: mariajesus.delgado@urjc.es; Tel.: +34-91-4887752

Received: 27 February 2019; Accepted: 26 March 2019; Published: 30 March 2019

Abstract: The goal of the present research is to contribute to the detection of tax fraud concerning personal income tax returns (IRPF, in Spanish) filed in Spain, through the use of Machine Learning advanced predictive tools, by applying Multilayer Perceptron neural network (MLP) models. The possibilities springing from these techniques have been applied to a broad range of personal income return data supplied by the Institute of Fiscal Studies (IEF). The use of the neural networks enabled taxpayer segmentation as well as calculation of the probability concerning an individual taxpayer's propensity to attempt to evade taxes. The results showed that the selected model has an efficiency rate of 84.3%, implying an improvement in relation to other models utilized in tax fraud detection. The proposal can be generalized to quantify an individual's propensity to commit fraud with regards to other kinds of taxes. These models will support tax offices to help them arrive at the best decisions regarding action plans to combat tax fraud.

Keywords: tax fraud; neural networks; intelligent systems and networks; personal income tax; prediction

1. Introduction

The quantification and detection of tax fraud is a top priority amongst the most important goals of tax offices in several countries. The estimates regarding tax fraud at the international level reveal that Spain is one of the developed countries with a high level of tax fraud, exceeding 20% of GDP [1–3]. Despite the measures implemented to curtail this, to date, there has been no reduction with respect to the trend [4,5].

In view of the significance of the problems resulting from tax fraud, and bearing in mind efficiency, equity, and the capacity to procure money, it is evident that improving the efficacy of measures to reduce tax fraud is high on the list of tax offices priorities. Designing control systems for detecting and fining people who do not fully meet their tax obligations could be crucial to lessening the problem. Making fraud detection easier in addition to achieving higher efficacy with respect to inspections could result in greater levels of tax compliance. In this sense, although empirical studies have not corroborated an increase in tax inspections leading to a reduction in the number of tax fraud cases [6,7], the availability of tools to streamline and heighten efficiency, where checks are concerned, would be of help in the battle to curtail fraud. Also, the development of new technologies and the considerable increase in information available for fiscal purposes (big data) provides an opportunity to reinforce the work done by tax offices [8–10].

Accordingly, this paper attempts to make a contribution through research conducted on the application of Neural Network models to income tax returns samples provided by the Spanish Institute of Fiscal Studies, with a view to facilitating the detection of taxpayers who evade tax by quantifying an individual taxpayer's tendency to commit fraud. With this goal in mind, use was made of Machine Learning advanced predictive tools for supervised learning, specifically of the neural networks model.

A very significant added value of this study is the utilization of databases pertaining to official administrative sources. This means that there are no problems arising from missing data, nor other data flaws. The information used is the official data from the Spanish Revenue Office, (https://www.agenciatributaria.es/) implying their validity, tax analysis, and taxpayer inspection is based on the said data [11]. In particular, the IRPF sample utilized in this study is the main instrument for fiscal analysis.

Lastly, the methodology resorted to in this paper can be generalized to quantify each taxpayer's propensity to commit any other kind of tax fraud. The availability of huge data sets containing information on each taxation concept allows the utilization of a generic methodology to widen possibilities with regards to quantitative analysis and also to take advantage of the new services provided by big data, data mining, and Machine Learning techniques.

The structure of this article is as follows: The second section presents the background and describes the methodological approach applied in this study. The third section deals with the estimation and adjustment strategy. Additionally, in the same section, the sensitivity of the model concerning the entire training and sample is explored. The last section consists of a brief conclusion, in addition to detailing future research possibilities arising from the results obtained.

2. Background and Methodological Framework

In recent years, artificial intelligence has become a tool which permits the handling of huge databases as well as the use of algorithms which, although complex in structure, provide results which may be interpreted easily. This framework offers the possibility of detecting and checking fiscal fraud which is an area that has aroused the interest of researchers, and generated concern for public administrative offices. In this paper, the proposal put forward focuses not only on the utilization of neural networks for detecting fiscal fraud as regards taxpayers in Spain, but also on contributing to precise fraud profiling to facilitate tax inspections. From the literature, data mining techniques present several possibilities for data processing aimed at fraud analysis [12].

Neural network models normally outperform other predictive linear and non-linear models where perfection and predictive capacity are concerned [13–15]. From the quantitative perspective, they often consist of optimum combinations which permit better prediction and more accurate estimations than occurs with other types of models. The neural network facilitates classification of each tax filer as fraudulent or not fraudulent, and furthermore, it reveals a taxpayer's likelihood to be fraudulent. In other words, it does not only classify individuals as prone to fraud or not, but also computes each filer's probability to commit fraud. Hence, tax filers are classified according to their propensity to commit fraud.

Attaining the above-mentioned goal comes with a price due to software availability (suitable software for these techniques is not common), computation capacity (network algorithms are rather complicated and require adequate hardware for convergence), and methodological control (Machine Learning techniques are not trivial concerning methodology). To meet the objectives of this study, IBM software and hardware were used (www.ibm.es) to achieve the algorithm convergence of neural networks applied to millions of data and hundreds of variables. On the other hand, as any graphic representation which involves millions of points cannot be done without infrastructure which is appropriate for huge amounts of data, the same programming has been utilized.

We can define an artificial neural network as an intelligent system capable not only of learning, but also of generalizing. A neural network is made up of processing units referred to as neurons and nodes. The nodes are organized in groups called "layers". Generally, there are three types of layers: An input layer, one or several hidden layers, and an output layer. Connections are established between the adjacent nodes of each layer. The input layer, whereby the data is presented to the network, is made up of input nodes which receive the information directly from outside. The output layer represents the response of the network to the inputs received by transferring the information out. The hidden or intermediate layers, located in between the input and output layers, process the information and are the only layers which have no connection to the outside.

The most commonly found network structure is a type of network which is fed forwards or referred to as a feedforward network, since the connections established between neurons move in one direction only according to the following order: The input layer, hidden layer(s), and the output layer. For example, Figure 1 depicts a feedforward network with two hidden layers.

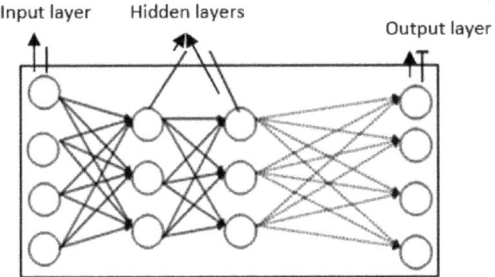

Figure 1. The general structure of a feedforward network.

Nevertheless, it is also possible to find feedback networks which have connections moving backwards, that is, from the nodes to the processing elements of previous layers, as well as recurrent networks with connections between neurons in the same layers, as well as a connection between the node and itself. Figure 2 illustrates a network model where the different types of mentioned connections can be found moving forwards, backwards, and also in a recurrent pattern, resulting in a fully interconnected network.

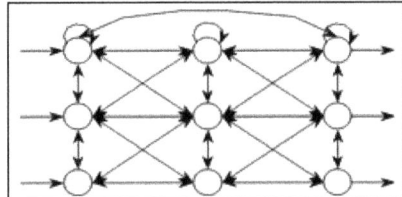

Figure 2. The general structure of a feedback network.

A fully interconnected neural network occurs when the nodes in each layer are connected to the nodes in the next layer. The sole mission of the input layer is to distribute the information presented to the neural network for processing in the next layer. The nodes in the hidden layers and in the output layer process the signals by applying processing factors, known as synaptic weights. Each layer has an additional node referred to as bias, which adds an additional term to the output from all the nodes found in the layer. All inputs in a node are weighted, combined, and processed through a function called a transfer function or activation function, which controls the output flow from that node to enable connection with all the nodes in the next layer. The transfer function serves to normalize the output. The connections between processing elements are linked to a connection weight or force W, which determines the quantitative effect certain elements have on others.

Specifically, the transformation process for the inputs and outputs in a feedforward artificial neural network with r inputs, a sole hidden layer, composed of q processing elements and an output unit can be summarized in the following formulation of the network output function for the following model (1) and in Figure 3:

$$Y = \hat{f}(x, W) = F\left(\beta_0 + \sum_{j=1}^{q} \beta_j G(x'\gamma_j)\right) \quad (1)$$

where:

- $x = (1, x_1, x_2, \ldots, x_r)'$ are the network inputs (independent variables), where 1 corresponds to the bias of a traditional model.
- $\gamma_j = (\gamma_{j0}, \gamma_{j1}, \ldots, \gamma_{ji}, \ldots, \gamma_{jr})' \in \Re^{r+1}$ are the weights of the inputs layer neurons to those of the intermediate or hidden layer.
- $\beta_j, j = 0, \ldots, q$, represents the connection force of the hidden units to those of pertaining to output ($j = 0$ indexes the bias unit) and q is the number of intermediate units, that is, the number of hidden layer nodes.
- W is a vector which includes all the synaptic weights of the network, γ_j and β_j, or connections pattern.
- $Y = \hat{f}(x, W)$ is the network output (in our case, it refers to fraud probability)
- $F: \Re \rightarrow \Re$ is the unit activation function and output while $G: \Re \rightarrow \Re$ corresponds to the intermediate neurons activation function. Selection of both was considered optimum, in accordance with the software utilized (It is normal to use the sigmoid or logistic function $G(a) = 1/(1 + exp(-a))$, which produces a smooth sigmoid response. Notwithstanding, it is possible to use the hyperbolic tangent function. In the expression $\hat{f}(x, W)$ if we consider that $a = x'\gamma_j$, we find that $G(x'\gamma_j)$ tallies with the binary logit model).

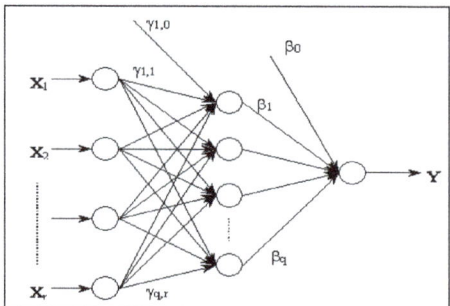

Figure 3. General representation of the network execution process.

As to the creation and application of a neural network to a specific problem, the following steps are shown in Figure 4:

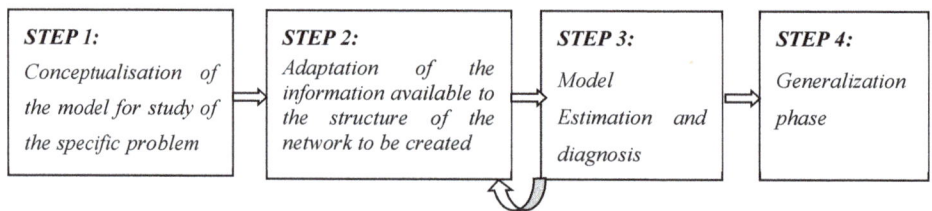

Figure 4. Steps in the empirical application of the model.

The neural network model we are going to apply in this study is the supervised learning model based on the multilayer perceptron. There are other neural network models such as the Radial Basis

Function (RBF), which is also interesting for this kind of analysis. Accordingly, it was utilized to compare its efficiency against that of the model presented, confirming that the multilayer perceptron provides the best results. The results obtained with the Radial Basis Function model are available upon request), given that it presents an output pattern or dependent variable which allows for contrasting and correcting data. Due to this, it is a technique used for classification as well as for prediction, for market segmentation, the positioning of products, forecasting demand, evaluation of credit files or analysis of stock exchange value, in addition to a countless number of other applications. Specifically, the multilayer perceptron stems from back-propagation error learning. It is the most frequently utilized algorithm, and besides, it mostly makes use of the backpropagation algorithm, the conjugate gradient descent, or the Levenberg-Marquardt algorithm. The advantages of the multilayer perceptron over other procedures can be attributed to the fact that all layers have the same linear structure, thereby rendering it more efficient.

3. Tax Fraud Modeling with Neural Networks

3.1. Data Matrix: IRPF Sample Provided by the IEF

For the application presented here, the data consists of the sample of Personal Income Tax returns (in Spanish, IRPF) filed in 2014 and which was obtained from the Institute of Fiscal Studies (in Spanish IEF). The sample consists of highly accurate data which is, moreover, characterized by an absence of problems related to infra-representation or the habitual lack in survey responses. With respect to the demographic scope, personal income tax (IRPF) returns filed in the previously mentioned year were used. The geographical area encompasses the Common Tax System Territory (excluding the Basque Country and Navarra). The period in question refers to 2014 fiscal year, bearing in mind that the samples had been compiled and published on a yearly basis, starting from 2002. Details pertaining to the methodology and the sample design, as well as the advantages and drawbacks can be found in recent papers [11,16].

3.2. Conceptualization of the Model: Application of the Tax Fraud Detection Model to Income Tax Returns

To build the Multilayer Perceptron supervised learning neural network model, the dependent variable used (single network output variable) is a dichotomous variable which takes a value of 1 if the individual in question commits fraud and the value zero cero if no fraud is detected on the part of the individual (mark variable). The independent variables (network input variables) constitute the most important items regarding personal income tax.

The purpose of the neural network model is to predict the probability any individual has to evade tax or otherwise, in accordance with the values declared in the variables included in Income Tax Form 100, available on the Spanish tax office website https://www.agenciatributaria.gob.es/AEAT.sede/procedimientoini/G229.shtml.

Taking this to be our point of departure, our ensuing analysis will enable us to draw up fraud profiles which could be of help during future tax inspections.

In this study, the independent variables used for the neural network model are considered to be the most important economic entries in relation to personal income taxation, as they are the concepts usually targeted by taxpayers attempting to evade tax. The entries in question include practically all the others as sum totals.

The following Tables 1 and 2 present the mentioned entries, which have been grouped in accordance with the different tax concepts: Independent variables, income tax minimum, and base variables:

Table 1. Independent variables of the neural network model.

Concept	Box
Earnings	
Gross work income (monetary)	par1
Net work income	par15
Capital gains gross income	par29 + par45
Capital gains net income	par31 + par47
Deductible net capital gains	par35 + par50
Gross property income	par70
Capital gains net income	par75
Deductible net property income	par79 = par85
Total deduction net income from economic activities under direct evaluation scheme	par140
Net earnings from economic activities under objective evaluation scheme (except agricultural, livestock forestry activities).	Par170
Net earnings from crop, livestock and forestry activities under objective evaluation scheme	Par197
Capital gains and losses positive net balance	par450 + par457

Table 2. Income tax minimum and base variables.

Concept	Box
Minimums and Bases	
General taxable base	par455
Savings taxable base	par465
Minimum personal and family, part of general applied	par680
Minimum personal and family, part of savings applied	par681
Liquidable general base levy on	par620
Taxable savings base on saving	par630
Quotas	
Central government tax	par698
Regional government tax	par699
Central government net tax	par720
Regional government net tax	par721
Self-assessment tax liability	par741
Tax payable	par755
Tax return balance	Par760

Reductions applied to the taxable base will also be taken into account:
We consider the total reduction applied to the taxable base to be the following variable:

$$\text{Taxable base rebates} = par470 + par500 + par505 + par530 + par560 + par585 + par600$$

Another significant group of tax variables correspond to deductions on account of housing, gifts, autonomous regional government deductions, investment boosting incentives, and other deductions. The applicable deductions have been grouped into variables as follows:

$$\text{Housing deductions} = par700 + par701 + par716$$
$$\text{Gift deductions} = par704 + par705$$
$$\text{Other deductions} = par702 + par703 + par712 + par713 + par714 + par715$$
$$\text{Regional government deductions} = par717$$
$$\text{Investment incentive deductions} = par706 + par707$$

Also taken into consideration are the total deductible expenses related to income accrued from work and from capital gains (par14 + par30 + par46), as shown in the following variable:

$$\text{Total deductible expenses} = par14 + par30 + par46$$

As to the dependent variable, due to the confidential nature of taxpayer data and the attendant legal requirements—which have been scrupulously adhered to throughout our research—the sample data on individual fraudulent and non-fraudulent tax filers follow the actual pattern without coinciding exactly with the concrete data. Moreover, the database used was completely anonymized. In practice, the fraudulent taxpayers would be those people in the sample that an inspection had determined, without a shadow of a doubt, to have been fraudulent.

Nevertheless, this research has been conducted independently of the year the data stems from since the goal is to find a methodology to obtain a tax fraud prediction function to enable quantification of income taxpayers' propensity to evade tax.

3.3. Dimension Adjustment: Reduction of the Dimension According to the Main Components

Our model features a series of quantitative independent variables, correlated with each other, that would trigger a multicollinearity problem in any model to be estimated. Consequently, it is imperative to reduce said variables to their uncorrelated main components. Adjusting the model to its components would eliminate the multicollinearity, in addition to reducing the impact of atypical values, and also bring about variable normality. Accordingly, after component adjustment, the model properties would be considered as optimum.

In this case, the reduction can be taken to be legitimate because the matrix determinant, relative to the initial variables correlation, is practically null. Moreover, the commonalities of the variables are high, with many of them close to the unit. As a result of the analysis carried out, we have obtained 11 C_i main components (factors), which account for close to 85% of the initial variability of the data, thereby securing a satisfactory reduction. In more specific terms, the components account for 84.882% of the variability, after a VARIMAX rotation.

Analysis of the factorial matrix revealed that the first component –C_1– comprises the first 17 variables, which include earnings, bases, and quotas. The second component –C_2– includes four variables related to the asset balances, tax and result of the filed tax return. The third component –C_3– encompasses 5 variables related to capital gains tax and savings base tax. The fourth component –C_4– contains 4 variables relative to fixed capital assets. Component C_5 comprises 2 variables, namely regional government, and gift deductions. Component C_6 comprises three variables pertaining to housing, and minimum personal and family deductions. Component C_7 involves a single variable dealing with economic activities. Component C_8 comprehends two variables related to taxable base and pension scheme deductions. Component C_9 contains 3 variables pertinent to total deductible expenses and investment incentives deductions. Component C_{10} is a single variable relevant to positive net balance, on account of capital gains and losses. Lastly, component C_{11} comprises two variables pertaining to the net return regarding agrarian modules and other deductions. Hence, the factorial matrix makes it possible to express each of the 11 main components as a linear combination of the comprising initial variables and in a disjoint manner.

The main components obtained are the input variables of the neural network model (independent variables). The output variable corresponds to the dichotomous mark variable, where value 1 indicates fraud, while zero value denotes the absence of fraud.

3.3.1. Multilayer Perceptron Network Model Estimation and Diagnosis Phase

For this research, feedforward artificial neural networks have been utilized, with r inputs (the most significant variables or income tax return items which are liable to be targeted for fiscal fraud), a sole hidden layer composed of processing elements q, and an output unit (fraud variable for indicating whether an individual has avoided tax or not). The network will make tax fraud modeling possible in the case of personal income tax returns and also permit assessment of an individual's propensity to fraudulent practices.

Estimation of the Multilayer Perceptron model, as depicted in model (1), was carried out with the 11 main components obtained in the previous section as the input variables, while the mark variable served as the output variable.

There are several advantages to using the main components as input variables in model (1). Firstly, the effect of the atypical values is eliminated since the component values have a far lower range than the initial variables. Given that the components are linear combinations of the initial variables, the effects of the atypical values are reduced. Secondly, data confidentiality increases since it is very difficult to identify individuals from the component values. Thirdly, multicollinearity problems in the model are eliminated because the components are uncorrelated. Fourthly, normality is induced in the model's variables due to the main components asymptotically normal behavior. Lastly, the predictive models with independent variables derived from a dimension reduction always adjust well, with a very favorable diagnosis.

In relation to the results obtained during the learning phase, 70% of the data was allocated to the training phase, while the other 30% were used during the testing phase. As to the number of rows in the database, there were approximately 2,000,000 in total, out of which 1,350,974 went towards training and the remainder for testing. There was no missing data in the database. The hyperbolic tangent function was used as the activation function in the hidden layers. The activation function in the resulting layer is the Softmax function. Finally, a sole hidden layer was utilized in the network, with a prediction percentage of only 15.8 percent for incorrect predictions during the training phase, and the same percentage in the testing phase.

Table 3 details the estimation results of the network's synaptic weights. The first seven columns of the said table estimate the synaptic weights of the input layer neurons regarding the hidden one (y_j), while the last two columns estimate the synaptic weights of the hidden layer neurons in relation to the output layer (βj).

Table 3. Estimations of the neural network model for tax fraud.

Predictor		Parameter Estimate								
		Predicted								
		Hidden Layer 1							Output Layer	
		H(1:1)	H(1:2)	H(1:3)	H(1:4)	H(1:5)	H(1:6)	H(1:7)	[marca = 0]	[marca = 1]
Input Layer	(Bias)	−0.274	1.639	−0.167	−0.122	−0.834	0.954	0.306		
	FAC1_1	1.173	0.029	−0.794	−1.110	−0.988	−2.318	1.828		
	FAC2_1	0.187	−0.319	0.649	−0.104	−0.278	0.508	0.430		
	FAC3_1	−0.035	0.488	−0.210	−0.490	−0.437	0.713	−0.514		
	FAC4_1	1.496	0.536	−1.207	−1.885	−0.466	0.200	1.700		
	FAC5_1	−0.101	0.157	−0.052	0.284	−0.298	−0.330	−0.074		
	FAC6_1	−0.098	0.467	−0.083	0.416	0.671	−0.892	0.898		
	FAC7_1	4.657	−0.763	0.750	1.847	−0.314	0.072	2.417		
	FAC8_1	0.289	0.889	−0.300	−0.342	−0.429	−0.245	−0.697		
	FAC9_1	1.272	1.280	1.850	−1.144	1.084	0.195	−4.070		
	FAC10_1	0.401	0.148	−0.022	0.181	−0.437	0.436	−0.833		
	FAC11_1	−0.541	0.164	−1.281	0.343	0.087	0.682	0.767		
Hidden Layer 1	(Bias)								−2.256	1.514
	H(1:1)								−2.131	2.104
	H(1:2)								−1.212	1.280
	H(1:3)								0.633	−0.874
	H(1:4)								1.102	1.594
	H(1:5)								0.911	−0.773
	H(1:6)								0.995	−0.860
	H(1:7)								−1.894	1.579

Figure 5 illustrates the structure of the neural network with the eleven nodes corresponding to the input or independent variables (main components), the sole hidden layer nodes labeled according to their synaptic weights, and an output node showing the two categories of the network model's dependent variable.

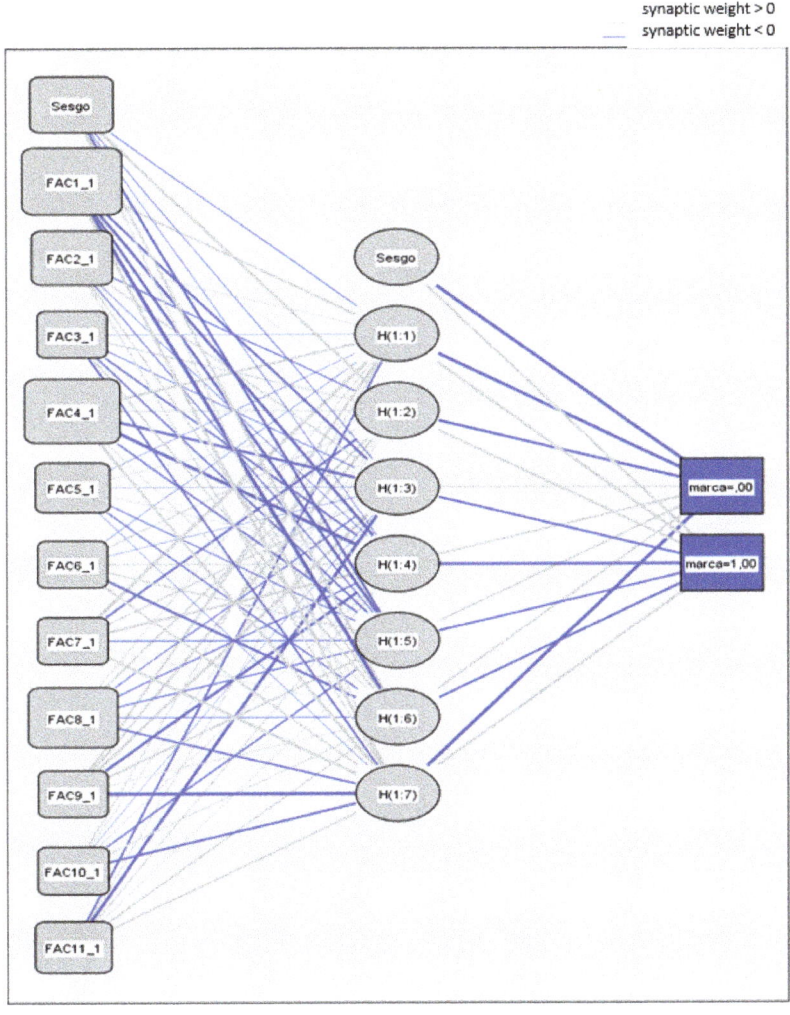

Hidden layer activation function: Hyperbolic tangent
Activation function of result layer: Softmax

Figure 5. Neural network structure for the model estimation.

The size of the input nodes indicates the magnitude of the effect of the corresponding independent variables on the dependent variable. Larger rectangles indicate a higher impact of the corresponding independent variable on the response. For example, the first, eighth, and fourth components have a greater effect on fraud. Be that as it may, the said effects will be numerically quantified later on.

On the subject of the network model diagnosis, in the first place, it can be observed that the confusion matrix, in Table 4, presents high correct percentages, 84% of global percentages for the variable dependent of global fraud, for both training and testing of the predicted values.

Table 4. Confusion matrix.

Sample	Observed	Classification		
		Predicted		
		0	1	Percent Correct
Training	0	441,525	63,016	87.5%
	1	150,694	695,739	82.2%
	Overall Percent	43.8%	56.2%	84.2%
Testing	0	188,867	26,963	87.5%
	1	64,279	297,411	82.2%
	Overall Percent	43.8%	56.2%	84.2%

Dependent Variable: fraude globle.

Additionally, the graphical elements for diagnosis or robustness confirm the validity of the model. As can be seen in Figure 6, in the network's ROC curves representing tax fraud or tax compliance, both reflect a very high area between the curves and the diagonal (0.918), pointing to the network's very high predictive capacity. On the other hand, the gain curve reveals a bigger width between the two curves for high percentages of between 40% and 70%, which confirms that the greater the gain for the same percentage, the more accurate the prediction. Lastly, the lift chart also confirms the predictive capacity of the model, as the higher the percentage, the better the prediction made by the model.

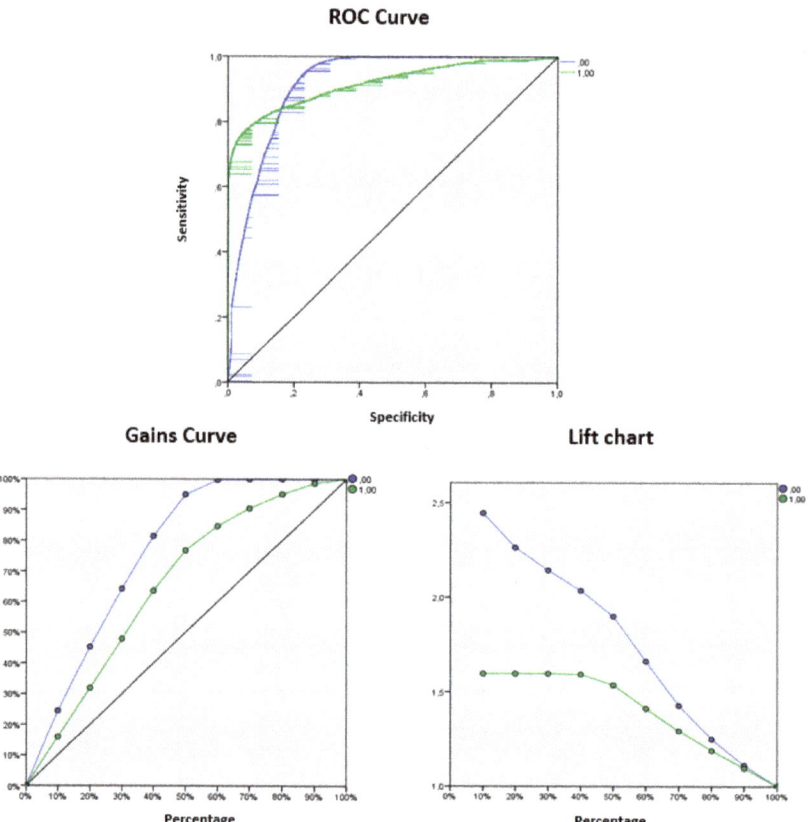

Figure 6. Model validation graphic tools. Source: Our own estimations.

3.3.2. Generalization: Calculation of Taxpayer Fraud Probabilities

One of the advantages provided by predictive models for tax fraud detection purposes consists of their utilization to calculate tax avoidance probabilities at the individual level. The neural network output classifies each taxpayer as fraudulent or not fraudulent, in addition to unveiling an individual taxpayer's tendency towards fraudulent practices. In other words, it does not only classify the individual according to their likelihood to commit fraud, but also computes tax fraud probability per taxpayer. Figure 7 illustrates the probability density of the propensity to commit fraud by means of the Multilayer Perceptron. It can be seen that fraud probability is denser for small values but also has high values of around 0.8 probability.

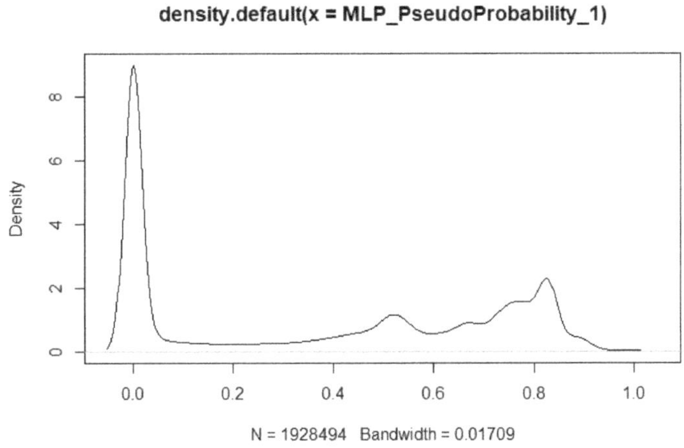

Figure 7. Density function for determining tax fraud probability. Source: Our own estimations.

On the other hand, not only do neural networks serve to classify persons with a tendency to indulge in fraud or not, but they are also of use for computing taxpayer fraud probability on an individual basis, and this is especially important for tax inspection purposes. Tax Inspections could be planned to include all the taxpayers whose fraud probabilities exceed a specified value or, at least, include a sample of such persons in case the resources available for inspection are insufficient.

The representation of the probability density concerning the likelihood to commit fraud obtained with the Multilayer Perceptron shows that the probability is logically denser for small values since there are considerably more taxpayers who comply with their tax obligations rather than those who evade tax. However, for fraud probability values greater than 0.5, we observe that the density increases up to values close to a fraud probability of 0.8. This fact indicates the existence of an insignificant pocket of fraud with high fraud probability values. It is still interesting to note that the density of fraud is higher for very small fraud values, as well as for high fraud values of close to 0.8 fraud probability. Therefore, we could refer to a polarization aspect of the likelihood to commit fraud.

4. Conclusions and Future Directions

By means of this application, it has been confirmed that neural networks offer low-cost algorithmic solutions and facilitate analysis, as it is not necessary to consider various statistical assumptions: Matrix homogeneity, normality, incorrect processing of data, and so on. Besides the advantage of the capacity of these models to modify the connection weights automatically, they are fault-tolerant systems. Additionally, the possibility of including all the information (variables) available in the model estimation and the speed with which adjustments can be obtained must also be emphasized. From the analysis carried out, it has been verified that the Multilayer Perceptron is useful for the classification of fraudulent and non-fraudulent taxpayers, and, also of use to ascertain each taxpayer's probability of evading tax. Furthermore, the 84.3% efficacy of the model selected is higher than that of other models. The sensibility analysis, conducted with the ROC curve, demonstrates the high capacity of the selected model in the matter of discriminating between fraudulent and non-fraudulent taxpayers. Thus, it can be concluded that the Multilayer Perceptron network is well-equipped to classify taxpayers in a very efficient manner.

Finally, the results obtained in this study present a wide range of possibilities to the improve tax fraud detection, through the use of the kind of predictive tools dealt with in this paper to find fraud patterns which could be described a priori, through sensitivity analysis. In the future, it would be of great interest to realize applications of this methodology in other taxes.

Author Contributions: Conceptualization, C.P.L.; Methodology, M.J.D.R. and S.d.L.S.; Software, C.P.L.; Validation, M.J.D.R. and S.d.L.S. Formal Analysis, C.P.L.; Data Curation, C.P.L.; Writing–Original Draft Preparation, C.P.L.; Writing–Review & Editing, M.J.D.R. and S.d.L.S.

Funding: This research received no external funding.

Conflicts of Interest: The authors declare no conflict of interest.

References

1. Herwartz, H.; Sardá, J.; Theilen, B. Money demand and the shadow economy: Empirical evidence from OECD countries. *Empir. Econ.* **2016**, *50*, 1627–1645. [CrossRef]
2. Herwartz, H.; Schneider, F.; Tafenau, E. One share fits all? Regional variations in the extent of shadow economy in Europe. *Reg. Stud.* **2015**, *49*, 1575–1587. [CrossRef]
3. Schneider, F. Estimating the size of the shadow economies of highly-developed countries: Selected new results. *DICE Rep.* **2016**, *14*, 44–53.
4. Barrero, F.D.; Laborda, J.L.; Sauco, F.R. *El Hueco Que Deja el Diablo: Una Estimación del Fraude en el IRPF con Microdatos Tributarios*; EEE2014-01. Madrid, Spain, 2014. Available online: https://dialnet.unirioja.es/servlet/articulo?codigo=5188642 (accessed on 27 March 2019).
5. Feld, L.; Schneider, F. Survey on the shadow economy and undeclared earnings in the OECD countries. *German Econ. Rev.* **2010**, *11*, 109–149. [CrossRef]
6. Barrero, F.D.; Laborda, J.L.; Sauco, F.R. *Fraude en el IRPF por Fuentes de Renta, 2005–2008: Del Impuesto sintético al Impuesto Dual*; EEE2015-14. Madrid, Spain, 2015. Available online: https://ideas.repec.org/p/fda/fdaeee/eee2015-14.html (accessed on 27 March 2019).
7. Mendoza, J.P.; Welhouwer, J.L.; Kirchler, E. The backfiring effect of auditing on tax compliance. *J. Econ. Psycol.* **2017**, *62*, 284–294. [CrossRef]
8. Alm, J. Measuring, explaining, and controlling tax evasion: Lessons from theory, experiments, and field studies. *Int. Tax Public Financ.* **2011**, *19*, 54–77. [CrossRef]
9. Almunia, M.; Lopez-Rodríguez, D. *The efficiency costs of tax enforcement: Evidence from a panel of Spanish Firms*. MPRA Paper. 2012. Available online: https://mpra.ub.uni-muenchen.de/44153/ (accessed on 27 March 2019).
10. Castellón, P.; Velásquez, J.D. Characterization and detection of taxpayers with false invoices using data mining techniques. *Expert Syst. Appl.* **2012**, *40*, 1427–1436. [CrossRef]
11. Pérez, C.; Burgos, M.J.; Huete, S.; Gallego, C. *La Muestra de Declarantes de IRPF 2009*; Working Paper 11; Instituto de Estudios Fiscales: Madrid, Spain, 2012.
12. Abdallah, A.; Mohd, A.M.; Anazida, Z. Fraud detection system: A survey. *J. Netw. Comput. Appl.* **2016**, *68*, 99–113. [CrossRef]
13. Anyaeche, C.O.; Ighravwe, D.E. Predicting performance measures using linear regression and neural network: A comparison. *Afr. J. Eng. Res.* **2013**, *1*, 84–89.
14. Dilek, A.; Caliskan, S. Comparison of prediction performances of artificial neural network (ANN) and Vector Autoregressive (VAR) Models by using macroeconomic variables of gold prices, Borsa Istanbul (BIST) 100 index and US Dollar-Turkish Lira (USD/TRY) exchange rates. *Procedia Econ. Financ.* **2015**, *30*, 3–14.
15. Tosun, E.; Aydin, K.; Bilgili, M. Comparison of linear regression and artificial neural network model of a diesel engine fueled with biodiesel-alcohol mixtures. *Alex. Eng. J.* **2016**, *55*, 3081–3089. [CrossRef]

16. Pérez, C.; Villanueva, J.; Burgos, M.J.; Martín, R.; Rodríguez, L. *La Muestra de IRPF de 2014: Descripción General y Principales Magnitudes*; Working Paper 10; Instituto de Estudios Fiscales: Madrid, Spain, 2017.

© 2019 by the authors. Licensee MDPI, Basel, Switzerland. This article is an open access article distributed under the terms and conditions of the Creative Commons Attribution (CC BY) license (http://creativecommons.org/licenses/by/4.0/).

Article
Sentiment Analysis Based Requirement Evolution Prediction

Lingling Zhao [1] and Anping Zhao [2,*]

[1] College of Computer and Information Science, Chongqing Normal University, Chongqing 401331, China; llzhao@cqnu.edu.cn
[2] Institute of Education Informatization, College of Teacher Education, Wenzhou University, Wenzhou 325035, China
* Correspondence: apzhao@wzu.edu.cn

Received: 12 January 2019; Accepted: 11 February 2019; Published: 21 February 2019

Abstract: To facilitate product developers capturing the varying requirements from users to support their feature evolution process, requirements evolution prediction from massive review texts is in fact of great importance. The proposed framework combines a supervised deep learning neural network with an unsupervised hierarchical topic model to analyze user reviews automatically for product feature requirements evolution prediction. The approach is to discover hierarchical product feature requirements from the hierarchical topic model and to identify their sentiment by the Long Short-term Memory (LSTM) with word embedding, which not only models hierarchical product requirement features from general to specific, but also identifies sentiment orientation to better correspond to the different hierarchies of product features. The evaluation and experimental results show that the proposed approach is effective and feasible.

Keywords: features prediction; sentiment analysis; LSTM

1. Introduction

The product feature requirements are the descriptions of the features and functionalities of the target product. This provides a way for a product developer to get and understand the expectations of users of the product. Product feature systems are undergoing continuing changes and a continuous updating process to satisfy users' requirements. Such requirements' evolution plays an important role in the lifetime of a product system in that they define possible changes to product feature requirements, which are one of the main issues that affect development activities, as well as product features.

However, the requirements of real product are often hidden and implicit. Product developers need to gather varying requirements from the users to know their ideas on what the product should provide and which features they want the product to include. Without the ability to discover these changing feature requirements from the users, they fail to make decisions about what features the product should provide to meet users' requirements. More importantly, in a real application, we need to identify the feature requirements of given products and the opinions being expressed towards each feature at different granularities from users. Taking smartphones as an example, some users care about general features such as appearance and screen size, while others may pay more attention to more specific features such as the user interface and running speed of the processor. On the one hand, different requirement information is interested in different granularities of features of a product. Analysis of specific product features and sentiments at a single granularity cannot capture the requirements of all users. We need to capture such different granularity requirements from user reviews. Therefore, it is necessary to convey the specific features and sentiments at different granularities of products to product developers so that they can easily understand the different levels of user concerns. On the other hand, the sentiment polarities of many words depend on the specific feature. For example, the sentiment "fast" is positive for the feature "processor", but it would be negative for describing the feature "battery" of a smartphone. Therefore, it is more challenging to model feature granularity and to incorporate sentiment.

Sentiment analysis is the computational study of people's opinions and attitudes towards entities such as products and their attributes. Understanding and explicitly modeling hierarchical product features and their sentiment are an effective way to capture different users' requirements. In this paper, we demonstrate the hypothesis for the task of hierarchical product features requirement evolution prediction by sentiment analysis with a recurrent neural network and the Hierarchical Latent Dirichlet Allocation (HLDA). It presents a hierarchical structure of features and sentiments to product developers or requirement engineers so that they can easily navigate the different requirement granularities. From the viewpoint of product developers, it is easy to capture the requirement information of different users on different granularities of product features. They can understand what users think of each feature of the product application by taking both the features and sentiment into consideration.

The approach is explored to discover and predict the evolution of different granularity feature requirements of the product from the users' review text. The approach combines deep Long Short-term Memory (LSTM) with the HLDA to predict product feature requirements of different hierarchies. The different hierarchical product features with their sentiment could be presented to a product developer as a detailed overview of the users' primary concerns with the information about which product features are positive and which features are negative, which is used to suggest changes in product requirements from users. It can be used to decide whether or not the feature is a candidate for a product requirement change. A product developer could easily obtain an overview of the product features from the whole set of review text by navigating between the different hierarchies. This could help them decide on the necessary changes to the product feature requirements.

The main contributions of this paper are as follows:

- We propose considering the hierarchical dependencies of features and their sentiments for product feature requirement analysis by combining the power of supervised deep RNN with unsupervised HLDA. This shows the potential advantage of a hybrid approach of a joint deep neural network and topic model;
- We use a hierarchical structure of product feature representations with sentiment identification to capture product feature requirements of different granularities;
- We investigate the effectiveness of hierarchical product feature requirements prediction over different pre-trained word embedding representations and conduct extensive experiments to demonstrate their effectiveness.

The rest of this paper is organized as follows: In Section 2, we review related work. The hybrid text analysis approach for product feature requirements evolution prediction is described in Section 3. We indicate the effectiveness of the presented approach by evaluation and experimental results in Section 4. The discussion is provided in Section 5. Finally, we summarize our conclusions and future work in Section 6.

2. Related Work

This work focuses on methods for requirements evolution prediction through sentiment analysis of users' online reviews. Several approaches have been studied to perform product feature requirements evolution detection effectively. We group related work into two categories: requirements evolution prediction through sentiment analysis and deep learning approaches for sentiment analysis.

2.1. Requirements Evolution Prediction through Sentiment Analysis

A number of studies have focused on requirement extraction for mobile applications [1]. Rizk et al. investigated users' reviews' Sentiment Analysis (SA) in order to extract user requirements to build new applications or enhance existing ones [2]. The authors analyzed users' feedback to extract the features and sentiment score of a mobile app in order to find useful information for app developers [3]. Guzman et al. presented an exploratory study of Twitter messages to help requirements engineers better capture user needs information for software evolution [4]. Jiang et al. used text mining technology to evaluate quantitatively the economic impact of user opinions that might be a potential requirement of software [5]. Guzman and Maalej proposed an automated approach to extract the user sentiments about the identified features from user reviews. The results demonstrated that machine learning techniques have the capacity to identify relevant information from online reviews automatically [6]. The analysis of user satisfaction is useful for improving products in general and is already an integral part of requirements evolution. An approach was presented for mining collective opinions for comparison of mobile apps [7]. To determine important changes in requirements based on user feedback, a systematic approach was proposed for transforming online reviews to evolutionary requirements [8]. A text mining method was proposed to extract features from precedents, and a text classifier was applied to classify judgments according to sentiment analysis automatically [9]. The authors proposed incorporating customer preference information into feature models based on sentiment analysis of user-generated online product reviews [10]. A semi-automated approach was proposed to extract phrases that can represent software features from software reviews as a way to initiate the requirement reuse process [11].

2.2. Sentiment Analysis with Deep Learning

Deep learning has been used for sentiment analysis because of its ability to learn high-level features and to find the polarized opinion of the general public regarding a specific subject automatically [12]. RNNs have been used for sentiment analysis by explicitly modeling dependency relations within certain syntactic structures in the sentence [13]. Besides these, Araque et al. attempted to improve the performance of sentiment analysis by integrating deep learning techniques with traditional surface approaches [14]. A knowledge-based recommendation system (KBRS) was presented to detect users with potential psychological disturbances based on sentiment analysis [15]. Irsoy and Cardie implemented a deep recurrent neural network for opinion expression extraction [16]. The work proposed a tree-structured LSTM and conducted a comprehensive study of using LSTM in predicting the sentiment classification [17]. Liu et al. proposed combining the standard recurrent neural network and word embeddings for aspect-based sentiment analysis [18]. Wang et al. introduced the Long Short-Term Memory (LSTM) recurrent neural network for twitter sentiment classification [19]. The latest research shows that attention and the dynamic memory network have become an effective mechanism to obtain superior results in sentiment classification task [20,21].

A number of research works have been proposed for supporting requirements evolution analysis. Previous research attempted to explore a machine learning model to discover software features and their sentiment simultaneously, which captures both semantic and sentiment information about software requirements encoded in users' reviews. However, our work differs from them mainly because we consider the dependencies of features and their sentiments. Most of the existing work so far has ignored the hierarchical structure of the features and sentiments, which assumes that all features are independent of each other. Although these existing methods are simple and commonly used, they suffer from the problem of feature-dependent sentiment identification from general to the specific. Knowledge about the relations between features and differentiation of the prior and contextual polarity of each feature are crucial. In order to better address this phenomenon, we convey it to a hierarchical structure in feature requirement analysis by using the combination of deep RNN and unsupervised hierarchical topic models. The joint model is able to capture inter-features and sentiments' relations without relying on any hand-engineered features or sentiment lexica.

3. Joint Text Analysis Model

3.1. Basic Framework

In order to model feature granularity and discover different requirements of users based on sentiment, we present a hierarchical feature requirement prediction method based on RNN and HLDA to solve the problem of hierarchical feature-dependent sentiment discovery. Figure 1 shows the joint model framework to present the basic working mechanism.

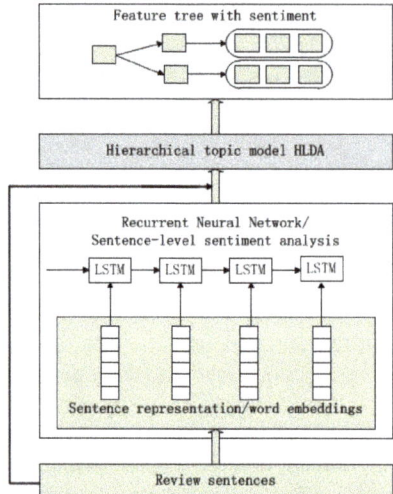

Figure 1. The joint model framework (LSTM+HLDA).

We introduce a recurrent neural network-based architecture that is able to learn both the feature-sentiment topics and the hierarchical structure from an unlabeled product review corpus. First, we use a component to identify sentence-level sentiment orientation by using an LSTM-based Recurrent Neural Network (RNN) with word embeddings. Intuitively, knowledge about the sentiment of surrounding words and sentential context should inform the sentiment classification of each review sentence. The sentiment polarity depends on the specific feature and context. This recurrent neural network-based component is able to consider intra-sentence relations to capture sentiment orientation.

Next, the second component is designed to identify hierarchical features, where these sentences with sentiment are fed to HLDA to discover hierarchical product features from general to specific to represent multi-granularity feature requirements. It is desirable to examine more fine-grained feature-based sentiment analysis of a product in more detail. This focuses on incorporating sentiment and modeling feature hierarchies to propagate the polarity of product features from general to specific. Thereafter, hierarchical requirement feature structure representation is generated with the corresponding sentiment, which contains more semantic information.

3.2. LSTM-Based Sentiment Analysis

In this subsection, we use LSTM-based sentiment analysis technology to identify the user's opinions being expressed towards each product feature. LSTM is a powerful type of recurrent neural network, which is to capture intra-sentence relations to provide additional valuable information for sentiment prediction. In our problem, we intend to use pre-trained word embedding in the LSTM-based RNN framework for the sentence-level sentiment classification task, which forms the basis for the next step to identify hierarchical features with sentiment orientation.

In the prevailing architecture of LSTM networks, there are an input layer, a recurrent LSTM layer, and an output layer. In the input layer, each word from sentences is mapped to a D-dimensional vector, which is initialized by pre-trained word embedding vectors. Given an input sequence of sentence $s = (features, sentiments)$, compositional context vector x_t is created by mapping each word token in s to a D-dimensional vector. This is designed to capture context dependencies between the features and sentiment of the sentence. The input layer can be represented as:

$$X = [h_{t-1}, x_t] \tag{1}$$

where the h_t is the vector of the hidden layer.

The LSTM layer connects to the input layer. The high-level compositional representations are learned by passing through the concatenated word embedding vector of the input layer to LSTM layers. LSTM incorporates "gates", which are neurons that use an activation function to remember certain input adaptively and are multiplied with the output of other neurons. It is capable of capturing relations among words and remembering important information for sentiment prediction. The LSTM-based recurrent architecture we used in this work is described as follows:

$$f_t = \sigma(W_f \cdot X + b_f) \tag{2}$$
$$i_t = \sigma(W_i \cdot X + b_i) \tag{3}$$
$$o_t = \sigma(W_o \cdot X + b_o) \tag{4}$$
$$c_t = f_t \odot c_{t-1} + i_t \odot tanh(W_c \cdot X + b_c) \tag{5}$$

where f_t, i_t, o_t, c_t are the forget gate, input gate, output gate, and memory cell, respectively. W is the weighted matrices. b is the bias of LSTM to be learned during training. σ is the sigmoid function. $\odot$ is element-wise multiplication.

The cell output units are connected to the output layer of the LSTM network for sentiment classification using softmax. We put the last hidden vector h_t of the representation of a sentence in a softmax layer.

$$h_t = o_t \odot tanh(c_t) \tag{6}$$

The probability of softmax sentiment classification in the output:

$$p(y_t = k|s, \theta) = \frac{exp(W_k^T h_t)}{\sum_{k=1}^{K} exp(W_k^T h_t)} \tag{7}$$

where w_k are the weights between the last hidden layer and the output layer. For sentence-level sentiment analysis, we use the Negative Log Likelihood (NLL) to fit the models from the training data by minimizing its value for the sentence sequence.

$$L(\theta) = \sum_{t=1}^{T} \sum_{k=1}^{K} y_{tk} \log p(y_t = k|s, \theta) \tag{8}$$

where $y_{tk} = I(y_t = k)$ is an indicator variable. The loss function minimizes the cross-entropy between the predicted distribution and the target distribution.

Based on such an LSTM recurrent architecture, we can capture sentiment information in the review sentence and identify polarities of sentiments.

3.3. Hierarchical Features Discovery

Hierarchical features discovery is to show a detailed overview of users' primary concerns with the information about which specific product features are positive or negative. For our hierarchical features and sentiments discovery of a product, we use the tree-structure model of HLDA [22].

Intuitively, a review often contains multiple product features and sentiments. Therefore, HLDA is reasonable to model a review text from a multiple product feature path. We feed review sentences with their sentiment from RNN into the HLDA to capture different granularity requirement features with sentiment orientation. The main motivation is to get the hierarchical product features and the feature-dependent sentiment, which is based on the assumption that a corpus of product reviews contains a latent structure of features and sentiments that can naturally be organized into a hierarchy. Formally, consider the infinite hierarchical tree defined by the HLDA to extract both the structure and parameters of the hierarchical tree automatically. The output of the model is a distribution over pairs of sentiment-feature for each sentence in the data. We employ the generative process as follows:

1. Draw the global infinite topic tree $T \sim rCRP(\gamma)$.
2. For each node Φ_k of feature k and sentiment terms in the tree T, draw a word distribution $\phi_k \sim Dirichlet(\beta)$.
3. For each sentence i in review document d:

   (1) Draw a feature-sentiment node $c \sim T$.
   (2) Draw a subjectivity distribution $\theta \sim Beta(\alpha)$.
   (3) For each word j

       i. Draw a word subjectivity $p \sim Binomial(1, \theta)$.
       ii. Draw the word $w \sim Multinomial(\phi_{k,p})$.

where $rCRP$ is the recursive Chinese restaurant process. This generative process defines a probability distribution across possible review corpora. Each feature and sentiment topic is a multinomial distribution over the whole vocabulary. All the feature and sentiment topics within a node Φ_k are independently generated from the same Dirichlet (β) distribution, which means they share the same general semantic theme. Subjectivity and non-subjective for each word indicate whether the word has sentiment orientation or not. With the extension of the HLDA model, the task of inference is to perform posterior learning to invert the generative process of review documents described above to estimate the hidden requirement features of a review collection. We use the collapsed Gibbs sampling method to approximate the posterior for the hierarchical feature sentiment identification model. The routine procedure of collapsed Gibbs sampling has been used in the Hierarchical Aspect Sentiment Model (HASM) [23], which solves a similar problem to our work in nature. Different from HASM, in our problem, we only need sample $p(c, p | w, \alpha, \beta, \gamma)$ for the feature and sentiment node c of each sentence and the subjectivity p of each word in a sentence.

The probability of generating sentence i in review document d from subjectivity p and node Φ_k is:

$$p(w_{di} | p, \Phi_k, \beta) \propto \prod_{l=0}^{1} \left(\frac{\Gamma(n_{k,l,-i}^{w,(.)} + \hat{\beta}_{l_i})}{\prod_w \Gamma(n_{k,l,-i}^{w,(w)} + \beta_{l_i,w})} \times \frac{\prod_w \Gamma(n_{k,l}^{w,(w)} + \beta_{l_i,w})}{\Gamma(n_{k,l}^{w,(.)} + \hat{\beta}_{l_i})} \right) \quad (9)$$

where $n_{k,l,-i}^{w,(v)}$ is the number of words having v_{th} vocabulary assigned to feature k and subjectivity l. n_{-i} represents the counter variable excluding index i.

Subjectivity sampling for each word is similar to the Gibbs sampling process in a basic LDA model with two topics: {0, non-subjective; 1, subjective}.

$$p(p_{dij} = k | w, p, c, \beta) \propto$$
$$(n_{d,i,-j}^{p,(k)} + \alpha) \times \frac{n_{c_{d,i},k,-j}^{w,(v)} + \beta_{k,v}}{\sum_{r=1}^{V} n_{c_{d,i},k,-j}^{w,(r)} + \hat{\beta}_k} \quad (10)$$

where $n_{d,i,-j}^{p,(k)}$ represents the number of k-subjective words in sentence i of review document d. n_{-j} represents the counter variable excluding index j.

In this basic extension of the HLDA framework, it learns the hierarchical structure of product features from review text. Not only topics that correspond to requirement features are modeled, but also the features are retrieved to better correspond to the sentiments. In this way, the resulting hierarchical features and sentiment provide a well-organized hierarchy of requirement features and sentiments from general to specific. This provides easy navigation to the desired requirement feature granularity for product developers or requirement analysts. As a result, the joint hierarchical model is an effective way to provide meaningful feedback to the product developer and the requirements engineer. It provides the descriptive requirement information to product developers by the navigation of product features and the associated sentiments at different granularities, which helps developers decide whether or not the product feature is a candidate for a requirements change.

4. Evaluation and Experimental Results

4.1. Datasets

The dataset is from an existing publicly-available Amazon review datasets (http://jmcauley.ucsd.edu/data/amazon/). This dataset comprises product reviews and metadata from Amazon, including 142.8 million reviews spanning May 1996–July 2014. Reviews include product and user information, ratings, and a plain text review, which has already had duplicate item reviews removed and also contains more complete data/metadata. We selected the app for Android review dataset among these to use in our experiment. The final app review dataset comprises 752,937 total reviews. The datasets were pre-processed by separating sentences and removing non-alphabetic characters and single-character words.

4.2. Experimental Settings

LSTM-Based RNN:

We used a fixed learning rate of 0.01 and changed the batch size depending on the sentence length. We ran Stochastic Gradient Descent (SGD) for 30 epochs. We set the hidden layer sizes (h) as 50, 100, 150.

Pre-Trained Word Vectors:

We used the publicly-available word embedding Google News word2vec (http://word2vec.googlecode.com/svn/trunk/). Mikolov et al. proposed two log linear models for computing word embedding from large corpora efficiently: (i) a bag-of-words model, CBOW, which predicts the current word based on the context words, and (ii) a skip-gram model that predicts surrounding words given the current word. They released their pre-trained 300-dimensional word embedding (vocabulary size of 3 M) trained by the skip-gram model on the part of the Google News dataset containing about 100 billion words [24].

Hierarchical Topic Model:

The HLDA model was set up to discover hierarchical feature requirements with positive and negative sentiment from users' review sentences. The Dirichlet hyperparameter of the HLDA was set as α of 25.0, and the prior was set as γ of 0.01.

4.3. Evaluation Metrics

We seek to assess whether sentence-level sentiment analysis based on the joint deep neural network and hierarchical topic model could provide support for hierarchical product feature requirement evolutionary prediction. To evaluate the presented approach, we applied it on the review dataset and chose to compare different review text content analysis models for requirements evolution prediction to analyze of our approach experimentally. The evaluation comprises two parts. First, we evaluated the sentiment analysis technique using standard measurements, and second, we evaluated the relevance and the effect of feature-dependent sentiment of the automatically identified hierarchical product feature requirements from the reviews.

The accuracy of the sentiment classification results from our model framework was used to evaluate the quality of the results. The Area Under the Curve (AUC) is a common evaluation metric for binary classification problems. The AUC value is equal to the probability that a randomly-chosen positive example is ranked higher than a randomly-chosen negative example. We used AUC to show the change in accuracy of sentence-level sentiment analysis under our joint model framework.

We utilized a further metric to determine the quality of the multi-granularity product feature generated by the HLDA. Product feature requirements relevance assesses how well the extracted text topics represent real product features, which show that the topics contain information that helps understand, define, and evolve the feature requirements of the product. Feature-dependent sentiment classification accuracy evaluates how well the extracted hierarchical structure represents a product feature, and the children nodes represent the sentiment polarities associated with it.

We evaluated both the requirements relevance and feature-dependent sentiment classification using precision, recall, and the F-measure. A feature was defined as a true positive if it was extracted from an online user's review by HLDA and was also manually identified in that review. A feature was defined as a false positive if it was automatically associated with a review in a topic, but was not identified manually in that review. False negatives were features that were manually identified in a review, but were not present in any of the extracted topics associated with the review.

4.4. Experimental Results

The different sentiment analysis techniques on product review enabled us to compare the results of similar approaches to analyze the effectiveness of each. Recent extensive studies have shown that the RNN-based sentiment classification method outperforms the previously-proposed sentiment analysis model. However, we mainly focused on comparison between the text analysis approaches, which are applicable to the requirements evolution detection from the online reviews. The Aspect and Sentiment Unification Model (ASUM) was used on user comments of software applications for software requirements changing analysis [25], which incorporates both topic modeling and sentiment analysis of the same model. Our evaluation compared the results with the ASUM text analysis approach to requirement evolution on the datasets. For each experiment, we evaluated the sentiment classification of requirement features from review text. We intended to evaluate whether the resulting hierarchical product features sentiment polarities classification could accurately represent the true sentiment orientation. The approach proposed in this work classified the multi-granularity product features extracted from the review text into positive and negative. This sentiment classification information can be used to detect the unique product features with the positive and negative user approval. In our framework, hierarchical product features sentiment classification was done by LSTM-based RNN. By comparing the product features sentiment classification extracted by our approach with the ASUM, we aimed to justify the effectiveness of integrating the deep neural network with pre-trained word embedding into the product features sentiment identification process. Figure 2 presents the results of sentiment classification on the dataset.

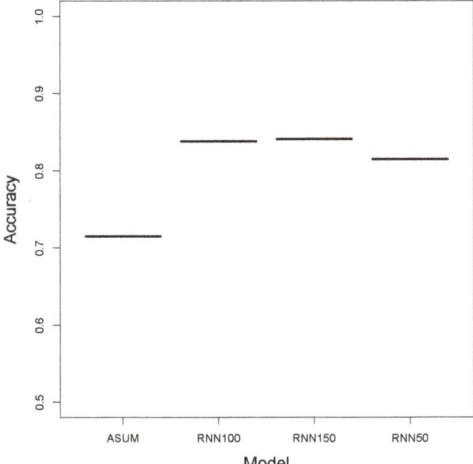

Figure 2. Accuracy comparison under the RNN with different numbers of hidden layers and the Aspect and Sentiment Unification Model (ASUM). RNN50, RNN with 50 hidden layers. RNN100, RNN with 100 hidden layers. RNN150, RNN with 150 hidden layers.

We can see that the relative accuracy of product features sentiment classification achieved using RNN with different numbers of hidden layers was better than ASUM. This may be mainly because of the feature sentiment classification methods having distinct characteristics. ASUM neither built any internal representations in a sentence nor took into account the structure of the sentence, while the RNN operated on sequences of words and built internal representations by word embedding before detecting the sentiment orientation.

We manually examined the 10 most popular extracted features for each of the 20 topics generated by HLDA to measure the feature requirements' relevance and feature-based sentiment classification. To compare the results of our approach with the manual analysis, we created a groundtruth set of product features referred to in the reviews and their associated sentiments. Following the previous studies, the content analysis techniques were used to create the groundtruth set [26]. Figure 3 shows the results of the relevance comparison under the joint model and ASUM.

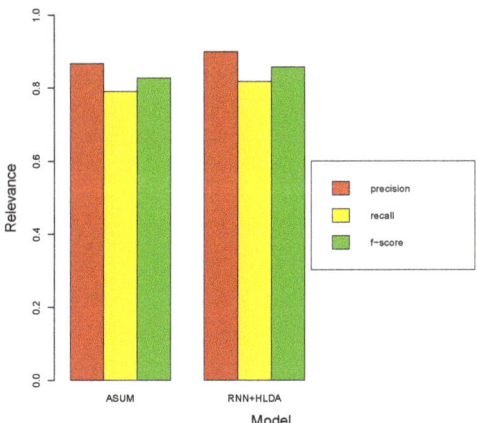

Figure 3. Relevance comparison under the joint model and ASUM.

We can note that the results were comparable for the two models. It can be seen that both of the models had good performance of relevance to requirements engineering for products. The extracted product features were usually words of topics describing actual product features. This is because both HLDA and ASUM identify the topics using models that are similar in nature, while the topics from the HLDA had different granularities.

The feature-dependent sentiment classification accuracy is shown in Figure 4.

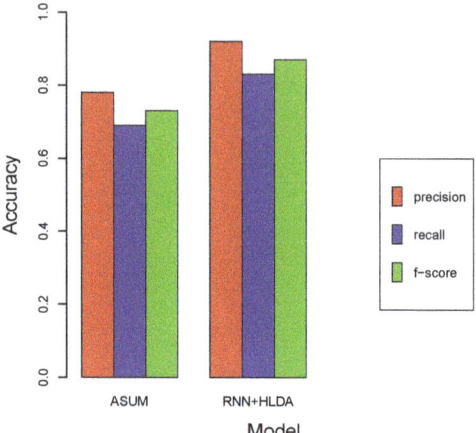

Figure 4. The feature-dependent sentiment analysis comparison under the joint model and ASUM.

We intended to evaluate whether the identified feature-sentiment hierarchy could show different sentiment orientations of some words depending on the specific feature at different granularities. The results of both the joint model and HASM show that the discovered feature-sentiment hierarchy can identify the sentiments for specific features and the associated opinions. We can see that the joint hierarchical model outperformed unsupervised HASM without any hand-engineered features. This may be mainly because of the distinct characteristics of sentiment classification. The LSTM-based recurrent neural network architecture was able to consider intra-sentence relations and provided valuable clues for the sentiment prediction task, while the HASM model, each feature or sentiment polarity as a distribution of words. This result confirms that the joint model was capable of analyzing sentiment for certain features at different granularities.

These automatically-identified features with their sentiment orientation are important for understanding how users evaluate the product, which might contain valuable information for the feature requirement evolution and maintenance of the product. To provide the experimental results as an example of the hierarchical product feature requirements presented in the user review, Table 1 is an example of the three-level hierarchical requirement features with sentiment orientation by combining RNN with HLDA.

Table 1. Hierarchical requirement features with sentiment orientation.

Hierarchy		Features and Sentiments
Level-0	features:	interface, update, power, usability, performance
	pos:	handy, could, pretty, friendly, usable
	neg:	frustrating, confusing, crash, fault, inconvenient
Level-1	features:	permission, log, option, connection, availability
	pos:	smart, install, graphical, adaptive, instant
	neg:	error, slow, boring, stupid, block
Level-2	features:	popup, buttons, text, account, login
	pos:	attractive, compatible, support, control, search
	neg:	small, missing, confusion, poor, useless

The result presented different granularity information for the hierarchical organization of features and sentiments. We can see that the produced hierarchical structure showed certain features and corresponding sentiments at various granularities. The hierarchical nodes showed the requirement features at various granularities with different feature-dependent sentiments. The sentiment word changed its polarity according to the specific feature. This hierarchical structure of feature-sentiment shows that general features became specific features of the product as the depth increased. The hierarchical features were relevant in the sense that they covered important features at different granularities of the product applications. The result confirms that the identified product requirement features were organized into a hierarchical structure from general to specific. Requirement feature-dependent sentiment polarities were obtained mainly because of RNN-based sentence-level sentiment classification being fed into the hierarchical topic model.

These evaluations and experimental results verify the effectiveness of the hierarchical feature requirements evolution prediction. The qualitative results show that the features automatically identified from review text described the overall requirement change of the products. As a result, we conclude that the combination of the supervised deep recurrent neural network and unsupervised hierarchical topic model is an effective approach to requirement evolution identification from users' review text. The above experimental results and analysis show that our proposed method is efficient, feasible, and practical.

5. Discussion

Our hierarchical joint model achieved results competitive with the software requirements changing analytical model of ASUM and the hierarchical aspect sentiment model of HASM. We highlighted the identification of hierarchical features and sentiments where this facilitates product feature requirements evolution predictions from users' reviews. In our work, hierarchical features requirement evolution prediction can be divided into two core components: supervised LSTM deep learning for sentence-level sentiment analysis and unsupervised topic modeling for hierarchical features identification. Thus, we analyzed the impact of different word embeddings, activation functions, and sizes of hidden layers for LSTM sentiment analysis and discussed a prior of the Dirichlet distribution for HLDA topic modeling.

Word embedding is a distributed representation of words, which is combined with a word and its context to represent a word as real valued, dense, and having low-dimensional vectors and greatly alleviated the data sparsity problem [24]. Syntactic or semantic properties of the word are potentially described by each dimension of word embedding. The semantic representation of sentences and texts was captured by the use of word embedding. Pre-trained embeddings improved the model's performance. Further, combining different pre-trained word embedding with deep neural networks brought new inspiration to various sentiment analysis tasks. We plugged the readily available embedding of sentences into the LSTM network framework and used it as the only feature to avoid manual feature engineering efforts for sentimental orientation classification. Polarity was predicted on either a binary (positive or negative) or multivariate scale using sentiment polarity classification techniques. The compositional distributed vector representations for review sentences were obtained by concatenating their word embedding representations. The resulting high-level distributed representations were used as the individual features to classify each sentence-sentiment pair. As a result, the LSTM network's performance can be improved by choosing the optimal hyperparameters of the dimension of pre-trained embeddings for the word and paragraph vector training.

The proper selection of the activation function is an effective way to initialize the weight matrix W to reduce the gradient vanishing and gradient explosion effect. The activation functions used in LSTM for sentiment analysis are sigmoid and tanh. The update of the state value is described as Equation (5) in the form of addition with the sigmoid and tanh function to solve the problem of long-term dependencies in LSTM better. The size of hidden layers in LSTM depends on the application domain and context. A model with many hidden layers will resolve non-linearly separable data. For the sentiment classification task with the deep neural network model, we assumed that the data required a non-linear technique. The introduction of the hidden layer(s) of deep LSTM network made it possible for the deep network to exhibit non-linear behavior. The different size of hidden layers in LSTM affected the results of the sentiment classification task. For hierarchical topic modeling, we made the observation that features descending from parent feature k must be more similar to parent feature k than features descending from other features, and there are more sparse features with increasing depth of feature k in a hierarchical structure. We used a prior of Dirichlet distribution β as a parameter to generate more sparse features with increasing depth of feature k of a hierarchical structure. The smaller the parameter value is, the more sparse the distribution is when the values of a parameter are less than one.

In light of the implicit expressions for product features and sentiment in the users' reviews, implicit semantic discovery is often preferred. Exploring better ways to incorporate such implicit information into word embedding representation, as well as methods to inject other forms of context information is thus an important research avenue, which we propose as future work.

6. Conclusions and Future Works

In this paper, we explored the use of the joint unsupervised topic model and deep LSTM-based sentiment analysis to identify hierarchical feature sentiment for requirement evolution prediction. The main motivation is to facilitate the product developers to capture and understand the requirements change in a navigable way between the different product feature requirement granularities. The results of this work significantly contribute to efforts toward automatic text mining analysis for product requirements engineering.

The methodology revolves around the sentiment analysis and hierarchical topic modeling technology to capture an overview of users' primary concerns. The approach was able to detect product features mentioned in the user review text for different granularities with sentiment orientation. The work presented here demonstrates the potential of combining deep neural network-based sentiment analysis with topic modeling for requirement evolution prediction from users' reviews. Our joint framework makes assumptions that product feature context dependent sentiment can be captured by learning compositional word embedding representations of corresponding features. Distributed word embedding can be different from the different training objectives and language models. Therefore, the quality of the word embedding could have an impact on the efficacy of the sentiment classification results.

Because of the many implicit expressions for product features and sentiment in the user's review, the text analysis-based approach to product requirements evolution detection should be adapted to the implicit context to identify implicit product features and sentiment. This is an issue worth investigating for our future work.

Author Contributions: Conceptualization, A.Z. and L.Z.; Methodology, A.Z. and L.Z.; Validation, L.Z.; Formal Analysis, A.Z. and L.Z.; Writing—Original Draft Preparation, L.Z.; Writing—Review & Editing, A.Z.

Funding: This research was funded by the Chongqing Research Program of Basic Research and Frontier Technology Grant Number cstc2018jcyjAX0708.

Conflicts of Interest: The authors declare no conflict of interest.

References

1. Nagappan, M.; Shihab, E. Future trends in software engineering research for mobile apps. In Proceedings of the 23rd IEEE International Conference on Software Analysis, Evolution, and Reengineering, Osaka, Japan, 14–18 March 2016.
2. Rizk, N.M.; Ebada, A.; Nasr, E.S. Investigating mobile applications' re-quirements evolution through sentiment analysis of users' reviews. In Proceedings of the 11th International Computer Engineering Conference (ICENCO 2015), Cairo, Egypt, 29–30 December 2015; pp. 123–130.
3. Guzman, E.; Maalej, W. How do users like this feature? a fine grained sentiment analysis of app reviews. In Proceedings of the 2014 IEEE 22nd International Requirements Engineering Conference (RE), Karlskrona, Sweden, 25–29 August 2014; pp. 153–162.
4. Guzman, E.; Alkadhi, R.; Seyff, N. An exploratory study of Twitter messages about software applications. *Requir. Eng.* **2017**, *22*, 387–412. [CrossRef]
5. Jiang, W.; Ruan, H.; Zhang, L. *Analysis of Economic Impact of Online Reviews: An Approach for Market-Driven Requirements Evolution*; Springer: Berlin/Heidelberg, Germany, 2014; pp. 45–59.
6. Guzman, E.; Alkadhi, R.; Seyff, N. A needle in a haystack: What do twitter users say about software? In Proceedings of the 2016 IEEE 24th International Requirements Engineering Conference (RE), Beijing, China, 12–16 September 2016.
7. Malik, H.; Shakshuki, E.M. Mining collective opinions for comparison of mobile apps. *Procedia Comput. Sci.* **2016**, *94*, 168–175. [CrossRef]
8. Jiang, W.; Ruan, H.; Zhang, L.; Lew, P.; Jiang, J. For user-driven software evolution: requirements elicitation derived from mining online reviews. In Proceedings of the 18th Pacific-Asia Conference on Knowledge Discovery and Data Mining, Tainan, Taiwan, 13–16 May 2014; pp. 584–595.
9. Liu, Y.H.; Chen, Y.L. A two-phase sentiment analysis approach for judgement prediction. *J. Inform. Sci.* **2018**, *44*, 594–607. [CrossRef]
10. Zhou, F.; Jiao, J.R.; Yang, X.J.; Lei, B. Augmenting feature model through customer preference mining by hybrid sentiment analysis. *Expert Syst. Appl.* **2017**, *89*, 306–317. [CrossRef]
11. Bakar, N.H.; Kasirun, Z.M.; Salleh, N.; Jalab, H.A. Extracting features from online software reviews to aid requirements reuse. *Appl. Soft Comput.* **2016**, *49*, 1297–1315. [CrossRef]
12. Rojas-Barahona, L.M. Deep learning for sentiment analysis. *Lang. Linguist. Compass* **2016**, *10*, 701–719. [CrossRef]
13. Zhang, L.; Wang, S.; Liu, B. Deep learning for sentiment analysis: A survey. *WIREs Data Min. Knowl. Discov.* **2018**, *8*, e1253. [CrossRef]
14. Araque, O.; Corcuera-Platas, I.; Sanchez-Rada, J.F.; Iglesias, C.A. Enhancing deep learning sentiment analysis with ensemble techniques in social applications. *Expert Syst. Appl.* **2017**, *77*, 236–246. [CrossRef]
15. Rosa, R.L.; Schwartz, G.M.; Ruggiero, W.V.; Rodriguez, D.Z. A Knowledge-Based Recommendation System that includes Sentiment Analysis and Deep Learning. *IEEE Trans. Ind. Inform.* **2018**. [CrossRef]
16. Irsoy, O.; Cardie, C. Opinion mining with deep recurrent neural networks. In Proceedings of the 2014 Conference on Empirical Methods in Natural Language Processing, Doha, Qatar, 25–29 October 2014; pp. 720–728.
17. Tai, K.S.; Socher, R.; Manning, C.D. Improved semantic representations from tree-structured long short-term memory networks. *arXiv* **2015**, arXiv:1503.00075. Available online: https://arxiv.org/abs/1503.00075 (accessed on 13 February 2019).
18. Liu, P.; Joty, S.; Meng, H. Fine-grained opinion mining with recurrent neural networks and word embeddings. In Proceedings of the 2015 Conference on Empirical Methods in Natural Language Processing, Lisbon, Portugal, 17–21 September 2015; pp. 1433–1443.

19. Wang, X.; Liu, Y.; Chengjie, S.U.N.; Wang, B.; Wang, X. Predicting polarities of tweets by composing word embeddings with long short-term memory. In Proceedings of the 53rd Annual Meeting of the Association for Computational Linguistics and the 7th International Joint Conference on Natural Language Processing of the Asian Federation of Natural Language Processing, Beijing, China, 27–31 July 2015; pp. 1343–1353.
20. Zhang, Y.; Er, M.J.; Venkatesan, R.; Wang, N.; Pratama, M. Sentiment classification using Comprehensive Attention Recurrent models. In Proceedings of the International Joint Conference on Neural Networks (IJCNN 2016), Vancouver, BC, Canada, 24–29 July 2016; pp. 1562–1569.
21. Kumar, A.; Irsoy, O.; Ondruska, P.; Iyyer, M.; Bradbury, J.; Gulrajani, I.; Zhong V.; Paulus, R.; Socher, R. Ask Me Anything: Dynamic Memory Networks for Natural Language Processing. In Proceedings of the International Conference on Machine Learning (ICML2016), New York, NY, USA, 19–24 June 2016; pp. 1378–1387.
22. Kim, J.H.; Kim, D.; Kim, S.; Oh, A. Modeling topic hierarchies with the recursive Chinese restaurant process. In Proceedings of the 21st ACM International Conference on Information and Knowledge Management, Maui, HI, USA, 29 October–2 November 2012; pp. 783–792.
23. Kim, S.; Zhang, J.; Chen, Z.; Oh, A.H.; Liu, S. A hierarchical aspect-sentiment model for online reviews. In Proceedings of the 27th AAAI Conference on Artificial Intelligence, Bellevue, WA, USA, 14–18 July 2013; pp. 526–533.
24. Mikolov, T.; Sutskever, I.; Chen, K.; Corrado, G.S.; Dean, J. Distributed representations of words and phrases and their compositionality. In Proceedings of the Advances in Neural Information Processing Systems, Lake Tahoe, NV, USA, 5–10 December 2013; pp. 3111–3119.
25. Galvis Carreño, L.V.; Winbladh, K. Analysis of user comments: An approach for software requirements evolution. In Proceedings of the 2013 International Conference on Software Engineering, San Francisco, CA, USA, 18–26 May 2013; pp. 582–591.
26. Maalej, W.; Robillard, M.P. Patterns of Knowledge in API Reference Documentation. *IEEE Trans. Softw. Eng.* **2013**, *39*, 1264–1282. [CrossRef]

© 2019 by the authors. Licensee MDPI, Basel, Switzerland. This article is an open access article distributed under the terms and conditions of the Creative Commons Attribution (CC BY) license (http://creativecommons.org/licenses/by/4.0/).

Article

Audio-Visual Genres and Polymediation in Successful Spanish YouTubers [†,‡]

Lorenzo J. Torres Hortelano

Department of Sciences of Communication, Universidad Rey Juan Carlos, 28943 Fuenlabrada, Madrid, Spain; lorenzojavier.torres.hortelano@urjc.es; Tel.: +34-914888445

† This paper is dedicated to our colleague in INFOCENT, Javier López Villanueva, who died on 31 December 2018 during the finalization of this article, RIP.

‡ A short version of this article was presented as "Populism, Media, Politics, and Immigration in a Globalized World", in Proceedings of the 13th Global Communication Association Conference Rey Juan Carlos University, Madrid, Spain, 17–19 May 2018.

Received: 8 January 2019; Accepted: 2 February 2019; Published: 11 February 2019

Abstract: This paper is part of broader research entitled "Analysis of the YouTuber Phenomenon in Spain: An Exploration to Identify the Vectors of Change in the Audio-Visual Market". My main objective was to determine the predominant audio-visual genres among the 10 most influential Spanish YouTubers in 2018. Using a quantitative extrapolation method, I extracted these data from *SocialBlade*, an independent website, whose main objective is to track YouTube statistics. Other secondary objectives in this research were to analyze: (1) Gender visualization, (2) the originality of these YouTube audio-visual genres with respect to others, and (3) to answer the question as to whether YouTube channels form a new audio-visual genre. I quantitatively analyzed these data to determine how these genres are influenced by the presence of polymediation as an integrated communicative environment working in relational terms with other media. My conclusion is that we can talk about a new audio-visual genre. When connected with polymediation, this may present an opportunity that has not yet been fully exploited by successful Spanish YouTubers.

Keywords: polymediation; YouTube; YouTubers; audio-visual genre; SocialBlade; elRubius

1. Introduction

The research on YouTubers, as a recent sociocultural and technological phenomenon, does not have a long tradition. This was the main reason for developing this research, which should be urgently completed because YouTube is a phenomenon that is decisively influencing contemporary audiovisual consumption and causing a series of dysfunctions in understanding audiovisual processing, production, distribution, and consumption. These dysfunctions are not necessarily negative, but I propose some ideas for more fluid short-term development. To do this, I propose a simple hybrid (quantitative and qualitative) analysis method, in addition to applying a theory of audiovisual media called polymediation.

In this paper, I present research that emerged from the research group to which I belong, INFOCENT (Información, Ocio y Entretenimiento/Information, Leisure, and Entertainment), at the Universidad Rey Juan Carlos (Madrid, Spain), that has been underway since 2017. This report is part of a research project entitled "Analysis of the YouTubers Phenomenon in Spain: An Exploration to Identify the Vectors of Change in the Audio-Visual Market", directed by the principal investigator, Álvarez Monzoncillo. In this research, we propose a methodology to analyze how the YouTuber phenomenon might be a new audio-visual paradigm that sheds some light on the tendency of audio-visual entertainment in the coming decades. The emergence of content creators on YouTube, whose profit is related to the number of views of their content and the new audiences that are migrating from classic media, is revolutionizing the viewing of audio-visual content on the Internet. YouTube is generating a new market formed by a worker-producer that generates content, an audience or public in some cases with interactive behavior (*prosumers*), advertisers who buy the advertising spaces of various formats on these channels, and a monetary flow related to this advertising. In INFOCENT, we analyzed this phenomenon through several work scenarios, some indications of research, and a methodology to address the subject, using mixed and transversal techniques that combine qualitative and quantitative research.

The main hypothesis (H1) that we address is that the consumption, creation, and distribution of audio-visual content generated by users (UGC or user-generated content) on the Internet, mainly on YouTube—popularly known as "YouTubers"—will not substantially change the context of the consumption, creation, and distribution of audio-visual content of the traditional broadcasters or OTT services in the short term. OTT or over-the-top refers to the delivery of audiovisual content streamed over the Internet without the involvement of an Internet service provider (ISP) in the control or distribution of the content. The ISP is neither responsible for, nor is able to control, the viewing abilities, copyrights, and/or other redistribution of the content, which arrives from a third party and is delivered to an end-user's device" [1].

Within this methodological framework, my paper is an original individual proposal, which is framed within the aforementioned research, that I have completed individually. My research shows a synchronous cut on a specific date: 5 May 2018. From this cut, I obtained a data packet extrapolated from SocialBlade, a proven tracking website of some relevant social networks. I explain this further in the method section.

In INFOCENT, we obtained clues as to how many aspects are changing in the traditional audio-visual consumption model: Generation of a community in permanent connection, new aesthetics and genres, new business models, increase in social disaggregation, nomadic and multiscreen consumption, omnivorous consumers, etc. These characteristics led me to use a theoretical concept—genuinely used in my own research—that, although recent, collects these in addition to providing additional theoretical value: Polymediation. This concept is related to the second hypothesis (H2) that we investigate: We think that the main YouTuber motivation is not the need, but the opportunity to provide content. So, the key factors of YouTuber success would be substantially different from the traditional factors: YouTubers focus on sharing a personal experience, creating a special audio-visual process, and building a trade name authorship, using for this any appropriations strategy, parody, pastiche, etc., which are factors related to polymediation.

This opportunity, given the need, is related to a certain narcissism or egocentrism present in social networks. Elsewhere, I analyzed the type of representation model that gives rise to this basic feature of the relationship of users (creators and consumers) with YouTube and other similar media [2]. As Ksinan and Vazsonyi claimed, there is a lack of consensus about how narcissistic Internet use impacts social relations, but this result could be due to the lack of differentiation between two distinct types of narcissism: A grandiose type and a vulnerable type, which function differently "with Internet behaviors and social outcomes". In their research, they concluded that:

The links between narcissism and social anxiety/social self-efficacy were partially mediated by preference for online social interactions (POSI); however, the two types of narcissism show distinct links to the two outcomes. Vulnerable narcissism was positively associated with POSI, which indirectly predicted problems for both measures of social relations; in contrast, grandiose narcissism was only directly and positively associated with social self-efficacy and negatively with social anxiety [3].

Here, I clarify that some of the success cases that I have recorded are categorized into this type of grandiose narcissism, whereas in other cases, this categorization is more problematic. All these successful YouTubers make this narcissistic exhibition a business by means of the monetization allowed on the YouTube platform. In this sense, this kind of business existed already in the origins of YouTube, with audio-visual characteristics originating in the prosumer, as can be deduced from this statement from one of YouTube's co-founders, Jawed Karim: "It was the first time that someone had designed a website where anyone could upload content that everyone else could view" [4] (p. 22).

Related to narcissism, but analyzing Youtubers from what Cocker and Cronin called the new cult of personality, they "differ from their traditional counterparts through collaborative, co-constructive, and communal interdependence between culted [sic] figure and follower", to the point that in Youtube, "the 'culting' [sic] of social actors becomes a participatory venture" [5]. Again, polymediation would be the key to shedding new light on the YouTuber phenomenon. This analysis could be applied to some of the success stories that I found in my sample, as the most famous in the Spanish case: elRubius. One of the keys can be found here: The emergence of many current YouTubers. As alleged by Levy, "it is no longer enough to have the American dream of fame and fortune ephemerally available to everyone—people want it on their desktops and on their cell phones" [4] (p. 167). Therefore, this narcissism, from the consumer side, would also be one of the YouTuber phenomenon success keys. Narcissism was analyzed in the same line by Ashman et al. [6] when they claimed that YouTubers "encourage a self-centered subjectivity where individuals pursue their own self-interest by seeking popularity at all costs" (p. 482).

Beyond this relative narcissism, but still related, other authors, such as Lange [7], discussed YouTube as a provider of videos of affinity, understood as all kinds of feelings of connection among the users (p. 73). It does not mean necessarily generalist videos—none of the success stories I found can be classified as such—but a "selection of audience" (p. 74). While for traditional television this would be problematic in success terms of translatable monetization, in this case, success is drawn from the wide audience, if one considers the diffusion of Spanish language in the world as virtually more than 477 million people speak Spanish as a native language, the second in the World after Mandarin Chinese, in 31 different countries, and 572 million Spanish speakers as a first or second language—including speakers with limited competence—and more than 21 million students of Spanish as a foreign language [8]. Also by the easy access, both by the interface and by not being conditioned by television programming. YouTube is also available indefinitely. One of the successful genres I have found that focused on video game commentary, or gameplay, is originally from the Internet era, and is related to this feeling of affinity. As Lindley stated, in gameplay, the YouTuber explains how they interact with video games, its rules, and how to challenge and overcome the games [9] (p. 183).

However, other authors, such as Ashman et al. and Berlant [10], balanced what is perhaps a too optimistic or naïve vision of the YouTuber world, as previous studies have not addressed the "three main wellsprings: The dynamics of competition, the creativity dispositif [sic], and technologies of the self" that "detrimentally affect the quality of their lives and collectively institute a 'cruel optimism' which promises much but delivers little" [6] (p. 1). This cruelty refers to the fact that YouTubers' work "links so tightly to their self-esteem—since it derives from doing something they deeply desire—yet the gains evidently manifest quite precariously" [6] (p. 482). I would say this is the case for most of the samples that I have examined in my research. In this sense, as I will show at the end of the analysis, and as Hess claims in a more political sense:

> The structural limitations of the medium of YouTube and the overwhelming use of YouTube for entertainment diminish the response. Ultimately, YouTube's dismissive and playful atmosphere does not prove to be a viable location for democratic deliberation about serious political issues. [11]

I have noted above how YouTubers' audio-visual production differs from traditional production. The most obvious difference is its distribution, as in this case, through a channel posted on YouTube. Even though several of the case studies that I review would seem to be amateur productions, they have millions of views. The democratization (lowering) of the media is not only shown in the production (video recording), but, above all, in the distribution level, because, as Bell et al. noted, "the mechanics and architecture of platforms, such as YouTube and Facebook, have provided a rich breeding ground for these types of cheaply produced content" [12]. In that sense, I agree with Burgess and Green [13] when they say that "the distinction between market and non-market culture is unhelpful to a meaningful or detailed analysis of YouTube as a site of participatory culture", as it is a platform with low entry barriers as YouTube provides a structure for what has always been the most complex, remote, and expensive custom of access for amateur production: Distribution and exhibition (p. 103). Thus, with the lowering of production costs, success only depends on the YouTuber knowledge, participation in the YouTube ecosystem, the savvy with which they produce content, and their mastery of YouTube's homegrown forms and practices (p. 104).

Duffy united both perspectives that I have been handling, one more psychological in its narcissistic conclusion and another more entrepreneurial, like the one I have just described. Duffy discussed neoliberal ethics and its implications, with a special interest in the case of entrepreneurial women—although they have a low presence in my body of work. Duffy draws attention to the gap among those who find lucrative careers and the rest, maybe dreamers, whose "passion projects" amount to free work for corporate brands as they:

> were motivated by the wider culture's siren call to *get paid to do what you love*. But what they experienced often fell short of the promise: Only a few young women rise above the din to achieve major success. The rest are un(der)-paid, remunerated with deferred promises of 'exposure' or 'visibility'. [14]

In the terms that I apply, this could be expressed as: Work to feed your ego—and maybe you will be monetized the remaining effort from that value. Duffy stated that "through the framework of *aspirational labor*, these women come to resemble the traditional media workers [...] they have defined themselves against [and finally] reaffirming the already-tight bond between consumption and femininity" [14].

These ideas were also reported by McRobie who analyzed the same dilemma as Duffy, also with a feminist perspective, but using professionally, Berzosa thinks about it as subjects focused on activities that were part of the public sector in the past (children, elderly, and the vulnerable caring). Finally, McRobie launched a question that, after analyzing the cases of successful Spanish YouTubers, is addressed in my conclusions as a sociopolitical reflection: Are the YouTubers and similar practices of creative labor able "to mobilize a new radical voice"? [15].

Beyond the feminist approaches in a medium as young as YouTube, one cannot lose sight of the fact that, as pointed out by Burgess and Green from cultural studies, YouTube is a media of "participatory culture", but the implications must be taken seriously because YouTube is considered to be their "core business" [16]. The idea was not originally introduced by them as Jenkins had already spoken earlier about this kind of participatory culture when he stated that:

> Circulation of media content—across different media systems, competing media economies, and national borders—depends heavily on consumers' active participation [...] a cultural shift as consumers are encouraged to seek out new information and make connections among dispersed media content. [17]

Despite this, Burgess and Green pointed to political contradictions and commercial culture mediation, born of an environment whose diversity in multi-platform digital distribution makes it difficult to call YouTube just "the mainstream media".

In the Ibero-American area, researchers, like Sabich and Steinberg [18], followed the same line as Burgess and Green and Jenkins, stating that:

The enunciation mechanisms typical of the *YouTuber* discursivity build a narrative structure that tends to professionalization, a form of multidirectional appearance of contemporary subjectivities and a specific logic of intervention, socialization and interaction in the Internet (p. 1).

What has already become popular both in academia and among YouTubers is the use of the concept of "communities" instead of a "social network", which has fallen into disuse for these cases of YouTube channels [19]. From this same perspective, Elorriaga and Monge [20] focused on the influencers of YouTubers subgenre, analyzing how there are some YouTubers, even starting from amateur positions, that have managed to shape communities and have necessitated "brands to re-invent their communication to keep connecting with their consumers". This is the case, for example, of the YouTuber, Verdeliss, a 33-year-old mother of several children who was successful among the Spanish YouTubers at the end of 2018.

This ability of the influencer YouTubers, as indicated by Pérez-Torres et al. [21], reminds us that, beyond the negative impact that I have pointed out above, the YouTuber universe is perhaps one of the most decisive for the creation of codes related to the construction of adolescent identity. As they specified, "most of the messages relating to personal identity were aimed at transmitting the self-impression of the YouTuber and the relationship of that self-impression with his gender identity, sexual orientation, and vocational identity [...]" (p. 1). Teen followers interact with YouTubers as one more expression of the fan phenomenon, adding to it by telling their personal stories. So, to understand the development of personality during adolescence—which is one of the age sectors that most interacts with YouTube—it is necessary to conduct further research into that interrelation. In this sense, "YouTubers are perceived by young people as their peers, but also with qualities (creativity or talent) that they often admire" (p. 69).

Ramos-Serrano and Herrero-Díz [22] delved into the influence aspect not as a subgenre, but as a basic characteristic of the successful YouTubers because they create opinion, and this makes them attractive to companies and the industry. They concluded "the key of [a YouTuber] success is the community of followers and that is why his future will depend on his ability to keep the balance between his specialization and the commercial content" (p. 115).

From an initial approach similar to mine, Scolari and Fraticelli [23] analyzed the production of the quantitative data collect from the top 10 Spanish YouTubers. They textually analyzed the five top videos of each of these YouTubers. I share one of their research questions: "What genres can be identified in the top Spanish YouTubers' production?" (p. 1). The date of the sample was 2 July 2015, so it will be interesting to see if some evolution in the audio-visual genres that they located has occurred. I only anticipate that two of the top 10 Youtuber channels are still listed in 2018–2019: ElrubiusOMG and vegetta777 (p. 11), which highlights the fierce competition in this type of entertainment channel. Besides, certain kinds of YouTuber audio-visual production are related to aesthetics and content "to satisfy the desires of a new generation of viewers formed in hypertextual experience" (p. 7). This brings us back to the concept of polymediation, which can be related to a concept that Scolari reflects on: Hypertelevision is something that shows screen fragmentation, acceleration of rhythm, intertextuality, rupture of narrative linearity, and multiplication of characters and narrative programs, comparing, then, the "old" and "new media" [24]. From this point, I diverge from Scolari and Fraticelli's analysis because I think that, beyond dealing with audio-visual products, the current media models are already radically different. One cannot talk about the evolution or adaptation of traditional media as these top YouTubers are new players in the future of the Internet. I agree when researchers claim that YouTubers, beyond uploading videos—virtually continuously, as a kind of *horror vacui*—do not just "create their individuality through those videos. Therefore, YouTubers should also be considered as 'media subjects'" [23,24] (p. 5, p. 8). This is another aspect in connection with the polymediation.

To summarize this literature review, since the emergence of YouTube in 2005, the academic literature has not stopped growing due to both its economic and sociocultural implications. In my analysis, I mix both perspectives focused on successful Spanish YouTubers. Several concepts are repeated, including narcissism, personality cult, affinity, and others unrelated to the technology itself: The business world and political freedom. There is also a sense of mantra, which is related to one of the concepts that I used in the title: Success. Berzosa thinks about it as if:

The successful YouTubers seem to share an element of truth and trust that makes them able to drag huge numbers of followers. A successful model from the point of view of the diffusion of the content, crucial for the creator to see satisfied their concern to impact in the audience, and also factor of enormous interest for the brands that follow closely this industry that, for some time now, struggles to produce formats with which to reach consumers better, in the age of *storytelling*, to tell stories to connect better with users, as well as to look for prescribers, influential profiles, with dragging capacity [25].

In my analysis, I show how most of this success is distributed equally among YouTubers that are basically dedicated to three audio-visual genres: Gameplay, reviews (specialized in certain subjects, especially for children), and fiction (short pieces of animations, miniseries, and memes). In this sense, I perceived a trend in the studies on YouTubers, especially in the first two genres and related to the participatory culture that I relate directly to the concept of polymediation.

2. Methodology

The method of analysis used in this paper is a hybrid between quantitative data directly collected from the YouTube platform, as well as from SocialBlade, a website of data gathering and visualization not only dedicated to YouTube, but to all kinds of social networks, like Facebook, Instagram, and Twitter, and a more qualitative approach in which I analyzed these data in response to a broad vision of the YouTuber phenomenon. I applied a synchronous cut on a specific day in 2018.

The body of work is composed of the 10 most successful YouTubers in Spain. The criterion of membership in this ranking includes the number of visualizations and subscribers to each channel, as well as the SB criterion from SocialBlade [26]. When this web was created, they just listed rankings based on the number of subscribers and the number of views, but it quickly became evident that this was not an accurate indicator of how people were actually doing on YouTube. Someone could have a bazillion subscribers that they cheated to get without having any actual views. The SB ranking system aims to measure a channel's influence based on a variety of metrics, including the average view counts and the amount of "other channel" widgets listed. If you have an A+, A, or A- SB rank, then you can consider yourself very influential on YouTube. This SB criterion is not totally accurate from a methodological point of view, but it can be integrated with some qualitative aspects that were of interest to me. In the analysis in Section 3, I expand on this idea and I propose some supplementary qualitative criteria.

Considering this ranking, the next step was to classify the members by audiovisual genres as well as by the age of the users to which these channels were aimed. In addition, I attempted to relate all this to the Spanish sociocultural context and examined, from a more sociological point of view, the possible deviations in the age ranges that could exist in the consumers of these channels.

Finally, after drawing this map, I related it to the concept of polymediation, which I explain in the next section. The map helped me to open up the qualitative research to propose new avenues of investigation that can help other studies related to YouTubers channels, as well as to their protagonists and users themselves in order to improve any aspect of this type of audiovisual structure.

Polymediation

Polymediation, as established by Madianou and Miller, is "an emerging environment of communicative opportunities that functions as an 'integrated structure' within which each individual medium is defined in relational terms in the context of all other media" [27]. In this sense, YouTube and the channels created by YouTubers are clear examples of polymediation, at least as far as its most basic structure is concerned.

From this perspective, Calka posed a question about how the media, identity, and our performance are related to an iconic saturated ecosystem. His research framed polymediation as a "discursive point of articulation for exploring the processes and outcomes of media convergence and fragmentation". That is, polymediation is a transition from thinking about the media as something one only consumes as one more product to understanding it as a process of which one has adopted. I think it is interesting to analyze this type of adaptation in the audio-visual genres. Calka sees it as:

> An opportunity for connection, invention, re-invention, and community, for bolstering and verifying aspects of our identity or playing with new possibilities for what one might become.

The complex relationship among media, identity, and performance is necessarily in flux. As our technological landscape changes, so will our identities and relationship to media. [28] (pp. 27–28)

Calka distinguished different levels of polymediation, which can best be treated under five key aspects [28] (p. 15–26):

(1) Ubiquity: Widespread and simultaneous accessibility and presence of media. From this, there are saturation phenomena of media platforms in our daily lives, the alteration in how information is sought, and how people connect with others and maintain relationships, while also providing many opportunities for distraction.
(2) Shape-shifting authorship: Multi-author mediation of messages in different contexts referring to the increasing power individual users must have in creating and distributing content; so, they are simultaneously consumers and producers.
(3) Simultaneous fragmentation and paradoxical merging or unifying performance of identity: A paradoxical fragmented/unified presentation, as users' presences online are all a part of who they are. These presences are performed specifically for others and are simultaneously fragmented as not everyone sees all these performances as they are intended for different audiences.
(4) Division and communality: Paradoxically, community is an extension of personal identity performance, but fragmentation does not prevent the possibility of communality, sometimes allowing us as individuals to engage with more communities that users might not otherwise be able to access without the technology.

Other authors, such as Madinou and Miller, understand polymedia as a new theory that can be used to understand the consequences of using digital media in the context of interpersonal communication [28] (p. 170). They understand a polymedia environment as an increasing number of communications technologies across different platforms that are used simultaneously or to complement one another. User identities across online platforms may be broadly similar or may shift in emphasis, from professional to social identity and among media. So, "the poly-media environment requires an individual's identity to perform different functions in a digital networked world" [29] (p. 25). However, it can happen as a communicative environment of affordances, not as a technologies catalogue. Thus, the primary concern of polymedia is to avoid the technological limitations and move toward the social interactions field, focusing on the emotional and ethical consequences. The reason for this is that each medium, with its different communicative possibilities, is deeply linked to the ways in which interpersonal communication through technology are experienced and managed. Some of those ways enabled by polymedia are "ultimately about a new relationship between the social and the technological, rather than merely a shift in the technology itself" [27] (p. 170). Madianou and Miller's main argument was that polymedia is about "a new set of social relations of technology, rather than merely a technological development of increased convergence" (p. 171). To understand this, they distinguished three preconditions: (1) Access and availability, (2) affordability, and (3) media literacy (p. 171). Polymedia is not just the environment, but is also how users relate to and develop these affordances, and how their emotions and their relationships flow (p. 172). Madianou and Miller posited that this flow or negotiation "often becomes the message itself" (p. 173). This means that it is not only about multimedia or media ecology, but is also polymediation of how the entire environment of different media affects or mediates between the media and the users.

Baym deepened the understanding of polymediation, highlighting seven key parameters: Kinds of interactivity, temporal structure, social cues, storage, replicability, reach, and mobility. Baym employed these key concepts to consider different facets of human communication, including the degree to which media is viewed as more or less authentic compared with face-to-face interaction; the sense of community, identity, gender, veracity, and the self; and how such factors work in various forms of highly personal or impersonal contexts for communication and the creation and maintenance of relationships [30].

Madinou et al. summarized polymedia as a transformation in technology and how users interact with it. People, traditionally limited to a couple of forms of media for communication, now have access to different media. However, the importance is not the number, but the new affordances and ways of using that offer temporality, storage capacity, reproducibility, materiality, mobility, and reach [27] (p. 183). There is a sense of re-socialization in media democracy and literacy, as users choose a medium as a shared social act. This is related to theories about mediation [29,31] or mediatization [32–34], which reflects the mutual shaping of social processes and the media and how to encompass the changes caused by the media into every aspect of our lives.

The concept of mediatization has its origins in the notion of replication, "the spreading of media forms to spaces of contemporary life that are required to be represented through media forms" [32] (p. 5). Both concepts come from the same theoretical background, but differ in application. Mediatization denotes the processes through which core elements of cultural or social activities assume media form. Therefore, those activities are relatively performed "through interaction with a medium, and the symbolic content and the structure of the social and cultural activities are influenced by media environments which they gradually become more dependent upon" [35] (p. 105). Mediatization highlights the independence of the media "with a logic of its own that other social institutions have to accommodate to". Simultaneously, these media "become an integrated part of other institutions" (id.). Mediatization also describes the transformation of many disparate social and cultural processes into forms or formats suitable for media representation [32] (p. 7). This (poly)mediatization is perhaps contradictory to the theories of globalization that hypothesize a flat world [36], as this cannot be alien to the peculiarities of each society. First, being a phenomenon that is already hugely popular, mediatization is far from reaching a significant level among the total potential users, at least in Spain. To discuss this unlikely globalization serves as an example in the cases of the Spanish Youtubers that I have chosen. I then wanted to examine how polymediation manifests itself in the Spanish case. For this, I analyzed the 10 most influential YouTubers using metrics from both YouTube and the qualitative data from SocialBlade.

3. Results

In 2016, I had the opportunity to visit Colombia to shoot a documentary in a mountainous area. In general, the landscapes and the people impacted me, but my most memorable moment was when, in a village with just one street, I met an eight-year-old boy interacting with his mobile phone. I was blown away by the discovery that he was a follower of elRubius, the popular Spanish Youtuber (Figure 1).

Figure 1. Colombian child using elRubius' YouTube channel, one of the most popular in Ibero-American countries. San José de Sumapaz (Colombia). © the author 2016.

The main objective of my analysis was to show the predominant audio-visual genres among the 10 most influential YouTubers whose content creation is completed in Spain. This top-10 ranking is extrapolated from a statistics website called SocialBlade.com, an independent website, whose main functions are to track social networks and offer statistics across multiple social media platforms. They are a leading provider of social media statistics that are freely available to anyone using their website. SocialBlade.com offers three different rankings about the most successful Youtuber channels worldwide, and by country: (1) Subscriber numbers, (2) video views, and (3) SB rank.

The SB ranking is provided because rankings based on subscriber numbers and number of views are not always an accurate indicator of what people are doing on YouTube. For example, a YouTuber can have many subscribers that can be fraudulently obtained without having any actual views. So, with the SB ranking system, you can discriminate these fake accounts, and measure a channel's influence based on various metrics. SB only assigns a channel an A++, A+, or A rank if it is influential.

This is a quantitative approach, but one that helped me to complete a qualitative final analysis. For this, I used the concept of polymediation that I described above. Polymediation is a term that refers to the numerous types of technology that users try and to the multiple ways in which they interact with technology. This summarizes the qualitative objective of my analysis, since YouTubers shape a kind of channel that is based on the fusion of different media and, above all, proposes a new form of interaction with users. From this perspective, my hypothesis is that YouTubers act as mediators between (poly)media convergence and users. I then examined how polymediation manifests itself in the Spanish case. For this, I analyzed the top 10 most influential YouTubers by combining SocialBlade's two quantitative metrics with their more qualitative metric.

The 10 top YouTubers in Spain sorted by the SB ranking are shown in Figure 2 [26].

			TOP 10 SPANISH YOUTUBERS (SB Rank, video views and subscribers)				
RANK	PREVIOUS RANK	GRADE	USERNAME		UPLOADS	SUBS	VIDEO VIEWS
1st	1st	A++	TheChacal547		327	1.309.702	743.362.797
2nd	2nd	A+	Doggy Doggy Play Doh Cartoons		579	3.373.087	1.140.161.424
3rd	4th	A	VEGETTA777		4.453	22.170.585	8.769.839.951
4th	6th	A	elrubiusOMG		774	29.040.242	6.534.933.987
5th	7th	A	Mejores Juguetes		1.144	7.543.489	5.117.727.840
6th	8th	A	Makiman131		2.264	7.054.122	1.622.131.642
7th	5th	A	Mikecrack		1.048	3.912.450	1.164.085.736
8th	11th	A	Las Ratitas		44	3,557,480	711,692,760
9th	9th	A	Doh Motion		232	1.711.937	185.062.395
10th	3rd	A	Oxiris		1.329	607.461	96.917.945

Figure 2. Top 10 Spanish YouTubers sorted by SB Rank.

Only one of the current Spanish YouTubers achieves a blue A++, *TheChacal547* [37], who created his channel in 2014 (Figure 3).

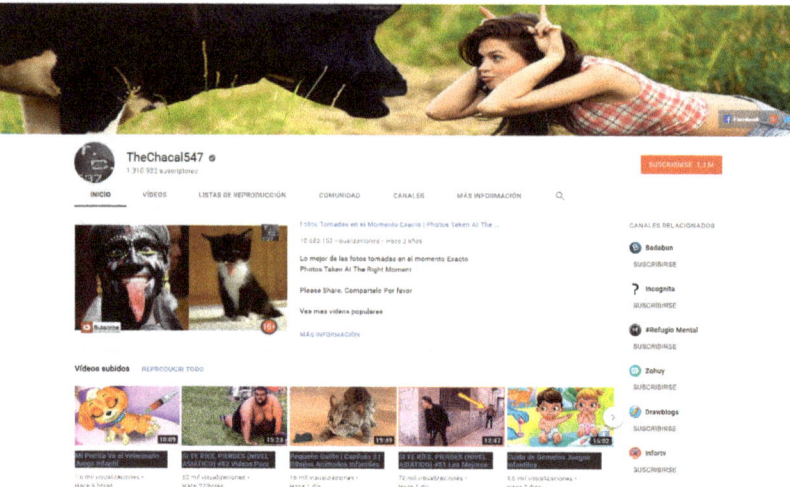

Figure 3. Front page of the YouTube channel, TheChacal547.

The only description of this channel is that it "provides the craziest and funny videos", which are commonly called memes and viral videos. This Spanish YouTuber is extremely successful since they are third at the global level as per the SocialBlade grading. In this first example, the predominance is already evident of a highly decanted content towards humor and comedy, in its most childish aspect. Polymediation is also evident: First, in being a specific channel, it has different content windows with both real images and animation, tabs for the community, and related channels and buttons to link with other social networks, like Facebook and Twitter. These qualities were replicated in all the samples of my research. The only other Spanish YouTuber that approaches TheChacal547 in the Social Blade rank is elRubius, albeit in position #279 (Figure 4) [38].

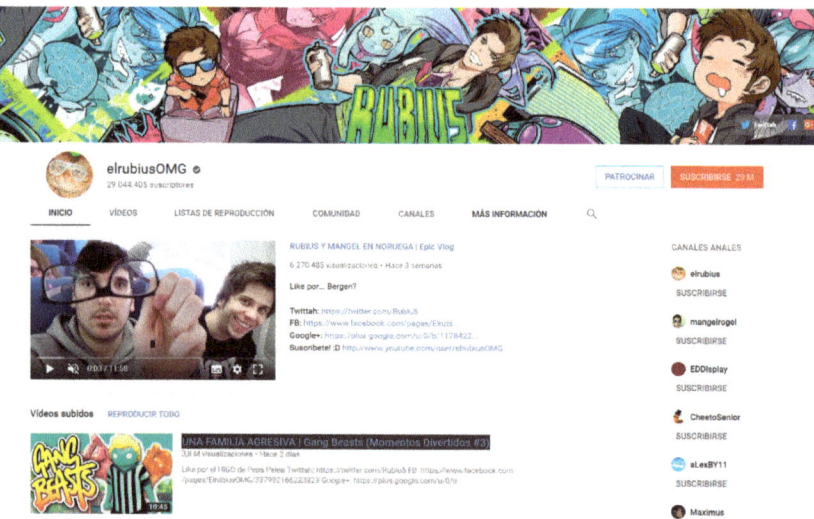

Figure 4. Frontpage of the YouTube channel, elRubius.

Considering the total number of world subscribers, elRubius is in 18th position, ranking 92nd in the world in video views (Figure 5).

10th	B+		HolaSoyGerman.		137	33,731,481
11th	A++		Canal KondZilla		709	32,556,108
12th	A+		Ed Sheeran		117	30,571,932
13th	B		Taylor Swift		161	29,882,181
14th			Popular on YouTube			29,792,990
15th	D-		Dude Perfect		175	29,678,386
16th	B-		Rihanna		69	29,364,090
17th	B-		Katy Perry		92	29,363,485
18th	A		elrubiusOMG		774	29,042,905

Figure 5. Youtuber, elRubius, in 18th position in terms of subscribers and 92nd in terms of video views worldwide. 5 May 2018.

On 5 January 2019, elRubius climbed up to 13th position (32 million subscribers) and VEGGETTA777 to 27th position (25 million subscribers). There were no other Spanish YouTubers in the global top 50. Some other Spanish language channels were listed: *HolaSoyGerman* (35 million subscribers) and their second channel, *JuegaGerman* (31 million subscribers), both from Chile, *Badabun* (31 million subscribers, Mexico), and *Fernanfloo* (31 million subscribers, El Salvador).

3.1. Video Views

The first chart (Figure 2) with the 10 top Spanish YouTubers is sorted by the SB ranking. However, when sorted by video views (Figure 6), there are some interesting changes.

			SOCIAL BLADE RANKING ACCORDING TO *VIDEO VIEWS*			
RANK	**PREVIOUS RANK**	**GRADE**	**USERNAME**	**UPLOADS**	**SUBS**	**VIDEO VIEWS**
1st	4th	A	VEGETTA777	4.453	22.170.585	8.769.839.951
2nd	6th	A	elrubiusOMG	774	29.040.242	6.534.933.987
3rd	7th	A	Mejores Juguetes	1.144	7.543.489	5.117.727.840
4th	10th	A	Antena 3	17.402	3.217.532	3.763.640.422
5th	8th	A	Makiman131	2.264	7.054.122	1.622.131.642
6th	5th	A	Mikecrack	1.048	3.912.450	1.164.085.736
7th	2nd	A+	Doggy Doggy Play Doh Cartoons	579	3.373.087	1.140.161.424
8th	1st	A++	TheChacal547	327	1.309.702	743.362.797
9th	9th	A	Doh Motion	232	1.711.937	185.062.395
10th	3rd	A	Oxiris	1.329	607.461	96.917.945

Figure 6. Social Blade ranking according to video views.

In this case, only VEGETA777, elrubiusOMG, Mejores Juguetes, and Antena 3 (TV channel) remain on the list. I discarded the latter as it adds distortion because it is a Spanish national broadcaster with a relatively professional and large team that are responsible for its content. VEGETA777 is a videogame-type channel as you can see on their website (Figure 7) [39].

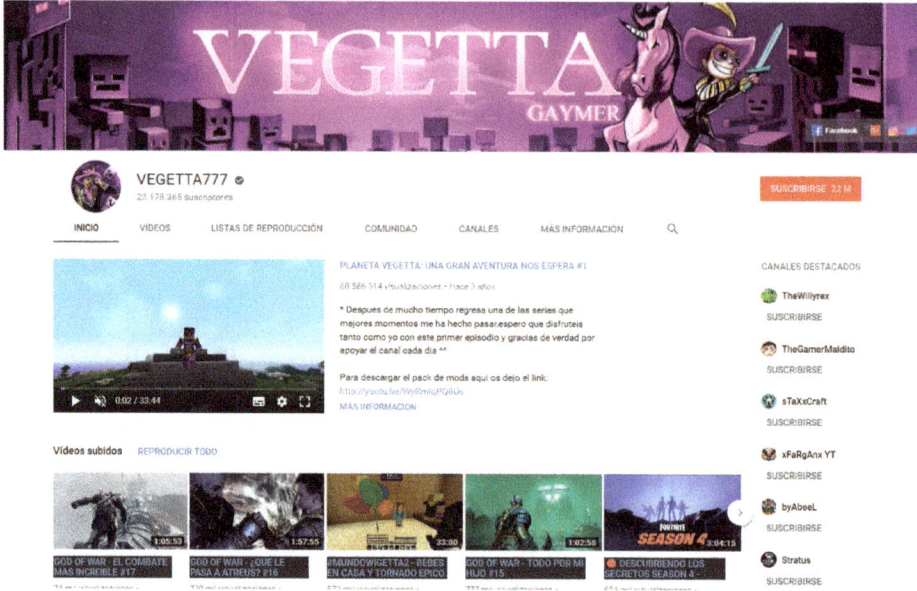

Figure 7. Front page of the YouTube channel VEGETTA777.

This is the description of this channel on their website: "♥♥♥♥♥♥♥♥♥♥♥♥♥♥♥♥♥♥♥ PURPLE UNICORN ♥♥♥♥♥♥♥♥♥♥♥♥♥♥♥♥♥♥♥♥". The channel description provided on the website is as follows: "This is a channel dedicated to video games directed by a guy [sic] who loves unicorns and lives with a killer elf in his room, if you subscribe to it you run the risk of falling into my madness, and it's not only me who says that, also the woman who appears at night on the roof of my room! A litle kisssss ^^".

There is a significant narcissistic syntactic structure in which he refers to himself in the third person and, without a lack of continuity, he starts using the first person. Again, an appeal in a naïve style is used to appeal to very young users.

The third in the ranking with more video views is *Mejores Juguetes* ("Best Toys" in English) [40] (Figure 8).

Since this is a channel for little children where toys are unboxed, the channel is a paradoxical case of this childish style, although in the description, she says that "it is an entertainment channel for children of all ages and *even for their parents*" [40]. The channel also has an animation series, *La brujita Tatty* ("Little witch Tatty"); but the creator, a woman who lives in Barcelona, keeps her name a secret.

Future Internet **2019**, *11*, 40

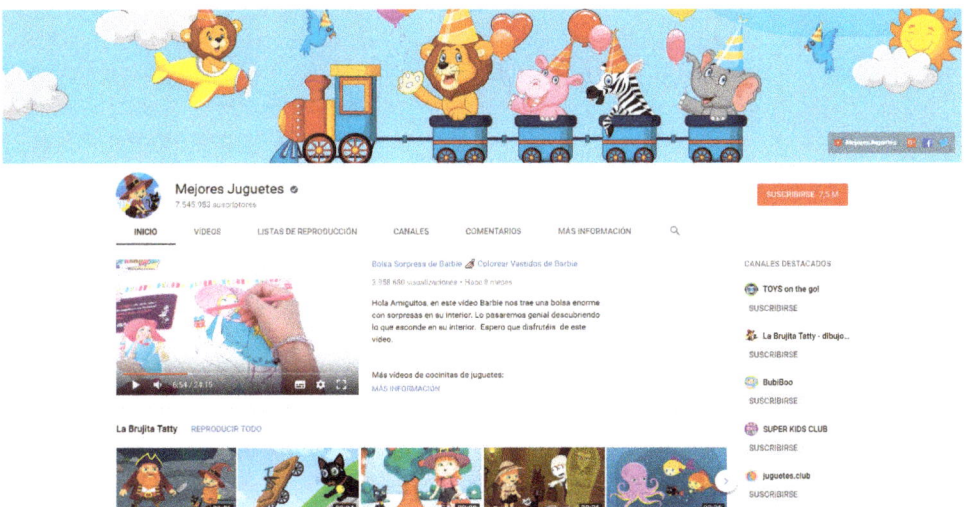

Figure 8. Front page of the YouTube channel, MEJORES JUGUETES.

3.2. Subscribers

Finally, regarding the number of subscribers, the majority of YouTubers from the original *SocialBlade* ranking disappear: Only elRubius and VEGETTA777 remain (Figure 9).

RANK	PREVIOUS RANK	GRADE	USERNAME		UPLOADS	SUBS	VIDEO VIEWS
1st	6th	A	elrubiusOMG		774	29.040.242	6.534.933.987
2n	4th	A	VEGETTA777		4.453	22.170.585	8.769.839.951
3rd	7th	A	Mejores Juguetes		1.144	7.543.489	5.117.727.840
4th	8th	A	Makiman131		2.264	7.054.122	1.622.131.642
5th	5th	A	Mikecrack		1.048	3.912.450	1.164.085.736
6th	2nd	A+	Doggy Doggy Play Doh Cartoons		579	3.373.087	1.140.161.424
7th	10th	A	Antena 3		17.402	3.217.532	3.763.640.422
8th	9th	A	Doh Motion		232	1.711.937	185.062.395
9th	1st	A++	TheChacal547		327	1.309.702	743.362.797
10th	3rd	A	Oxiris		1.329	607.461	96.917.945

Figure 9. Social Blade ranking according to subscribers. Source: SocialBlade.com.

The key problem with this methodology is that it introduces distortions, like the aforementioned Antena 3, and does not resolve the problem of the weighting between video views and subscribers. So, I propose to cross all three possibilities without that kind of distortion, and to give preference to the SB rank according to their highest rank: A++ and A+. From this point on, I focus on video downloads and the number of subscribers, which is probably the most easily manipulated criterion. From this mixed method, I obtained a list of the 10 most relevant youtubers in Spain (Figure 10).

			TOP 10 SPANISH YOUTUBERS (SB Rank, video views and subscribers)				
RANK	**PREVIOUS RANK**	**GRADE**	**USERNAME**		**UPLOADS**	**SUBS**	**VIDEO VIEWS**
1st	1st	A++	TheChacal547		327	1.309.702	743.362.797
2nd	2nd	A+	Doggy Doggy Play Doh Cartoons		579	3.373.087	1.140.161.424
3rd	4th	A	VEGETTA777		4.453	22.170.585	8.769.839.951
4th	6th	A	elrubiusOMG		774	29.040.242	6.534.933.987
5th	7th	A	Mejores Juguetes		1.144	7.543.489	5.117.727.840
6th	8th	A	Makiman131		2.264	7.054.122	1.622.131.642
7th	5th	A	Mikecrack		1.048	3.912.450	1.164.085.736
8th	11th	A	Las Ratitas		44	3,557,480	711,692,760
9th	9th	A	Doh Motion		232	1.711.937	185.062.395
10th	3rd	A	Oxiris		1.329	607.461	96.917.945

Figure 10. Social Blade ranking of 10 top Spanish YouTubers in descending order: SB Rank, video views, and subscribers.

The list in Figure 10 is a much more balanced list. In purple are the YouTubers that rise with respect to the original SB chart, and in red are those that descend. To even better balance the evolution of each Youtuber in these results, it would be helpful have the total visualizations since each one of these channels was created. In this case, the data are offered directly by YouTube (Figure 11).

In this case, the top ranked channel is VEGETTA777 closely followed by elRubius. However, the latter channel was three years younger (as of 5 May 2018) and only had 775 videos against the 4453 of the first. However, elRubius has seven million more subscribers. The YouTuber that follows in the ranking, Mejores Juguetes, has only one-third of the subscribers of the first two with only 1500 million views less than elRubius and the former was created three years later than this one.

The oldest channel—the first in the ranking—was created only 10 years ago, and the average age of these successful channels is approximately 4.5 years.

As for the evolution during the nine months since making the synchronous cut until 5 January 2019, the majority of cases are consistent in the first three positions: A growth of about 1%—2% per month in both subscribers and views, which accounts for the maturity of these channels in the top of the ranking. However, from fourth place down, the variability is much greater, with *Mikecrack* doubling the figures, or *Doggy Doggy Play Doh Cartoons* and *Las Ratitas* tripling these.

Finally, this table provides a current map of the audiovisual genres: The top positions belong to the stable non-child video games genre (meaning that they are aimed at adults). From the third position on, considerable variability is observed, with a clear tendency toward childish genres. I then examined this more closely.

RANK	USERNAME		UPLOADS 5 May 2018	UPLOADS 5 January 2019	SUBSCRIBERS 5 May 2018	SUBSCRIBERS 5 January 2019	VIDEO VIEWS 5 May 2018	VIDEO VIEWS 5 January 2019	DATE OF INCORPORATION
1st	VEGETTA777		4.453	4.952	22.170.585	25.320.376	8.769.839.951	9.859.440.642	2 March 2008
2nd	elrubiusOMG		774	787	29.040.242	32.821.111	6.534.933.987	7.194.939.080	19 December 2011
3rd	Mejores Juguetes		1.144	1.245	7.543.489	9.552.666	5.117.727.840	5.917.364.889	13 May 2014
4th	Makiman131		2.264	2.413	7.054.122	10.287.730	1.622.131.642	2.387.300.190	11 February 2013
5th	Mikecrack		1.048	1.187	3.912.450	8.106.411	1.164.085.736	2.519.580.577	13 July 2015
6th	Doggy Doggy Play Doh Cartoons		579	1.302	3.373.087	12.907.555	1.140.161.424	4.393.166.417	11 Dec. 2012
7th	TheChacal547		327	363	1.309.702	2.532.116	743.362.797	654.964.522	14 April 2014
8th	Las Ratitas		44	119	3.557.480	9.222.424	711.692.760	2.365.002.321	18 October 2015
9th	Doh Motion		232	140	1.711.937	1.849.609	185.062.395	73.070.975	24 May 2016
10th	Oxiris		1.329	1.311	607.461	601.768	96.917.945	99.300.733	19 August 2013

Figure 11. Rank per total number of video views on 5 May 2018 of 10 top Spanish YouTubers in descending order. Source: YouTube.

3.3. YouTubers Genres

Socialblade.com uses these eight categories or macro-genres that would cover virtually all YouTuber content: (1) Autos and vehicles, (2) comedy, (3) education, (4) entertainment, (5) film, (6) gaming, (7) science and technology, and (8) shows. From these, only entertainment appears in the 10 Top Spanish YouTubers. To be more specific, I propose the subgenres that can be deduced from this group: (1) Memes (fiction and reality), (2) children (commercial products and videogames for children, gaming), and (3) videogame (gaming not only for children). These three sub-genres could be classified into the traditional genre of comedy. For this, I propose the chart provided in Table 1.

Table 1. Subgenres inside the entertainment SB genre in top 10 Spanish YouTubers (5 May 2018).

	Memes	Children Videos/Video Games	Video Games
	TheChacal547	Doggy Doggy Play Doh Cartoons	VEGETTA777
	elRubiusOMG	Mejores juguetes	elRubiusOMG
	Makiman131	Mikecrack	Oxiris
		Las Ratitas	
		Doh Motion	
SUBSCRIBERS	37,492,931	20,258,331	51,818,288
VIDEO VIEWS	2,365,494,439	8,318,730,155	15,401,691,883

I also propose a tentative age distribution assuming that SB does not offer this service. Three large age groups were established: Young, adult, and old. I was then most interested in the thresholds, whose typology for the youth were divided into childhood (up to five years old), puberty or middle childhood (up to 12—14 years), and adolescence (until 19 or 20 years old) [41]. Therefore, given the generic content I analyzed, halfway between childhood and puberty may be a good limit, and this could specifically be eight years of age (Table 2).

Table 2. Tentative age distribution according to the number of subscribers and video views in the top 10 Spanish YouTubers (5 May 2018).

	<8 Years	>8 Years
	Doggy Doggy Play Doh Cartoons	TheChacal547
	Mejores juguetes	elRubiusOMG
	Mikecrack	VEGETTA777
	Las Ratitas	Oxiris
	Doh Motion	Makiman131
Subscribers	20.098.443	60.182.112
Video Views	8.318.730.155	17.767.186.322

Note that the difference among the subscribers and video views is because, in Table 2, I included some of the Youtuber channels from several subgenres, as is the case of elRubiusOMG, since this channel is mainly dedicated to the commentary of videogames and to broadcasting the experience of elRubius himself playing. However, memes also have some weight in the total content, so it was difficult to classify the channel in a single sub-genre. The total number of subscribers by genre is provided in Table 3.

Table 3. Total number of subscribers per genre in the top 10 Spanish YouTubers (5 May 2018).

	Memes	Children Videos/Videogames	Videogames
	TheChacal547	Doggy Doggy Play Doh Cartoons	VEGETTA777
	Makiman131	Mejores juguetes	elRubiusOMG
		Mikecrack	Oxiris
		Las Ratitas	
		Doh Motion	
SUBSCRIBERS	8,452,689	20,258,331	51,818,288

In this case, I added elRubiusOMG's figures only to the videogame column. The most important observation here is that the youtubers related to the videogames genre have the most subscribers: Almost double those related to children's content. The videogames genre could also be considered as being aimed at children; however, I think that the genre can be differentiated among the other main genres. An example is this photo captured from a video with 17,094,046 views [42] in the *Doggy Doggy Cartoons* channel (Figure 12), which shows the kind of YouTuber content that I think is exclusively aimed at children (under eight years old). The second picture was captured from a gamer video [43] published by elRubius (Figure 13), also childish, but maybe more aimed at children above the age of eight years.

Future Internet **2019**, *11*, 40

Figure 12. *Superhero Babies at the Supermarket Hulk Frozen Elsa Play Doh Cartoons Stop Motion Movies.* © Doggy Doggy Cartoons.

Figure 13. *La kill legendaria a Thanos/The Legendary Thanos Killing | Fornite.* © elrubiusOMG.

To argue my hypothesis about the childishness of successful YouTubers' content, the video published by *Doggy Doggy Cartoons* has almost four million more views than elRubius'. Perhaps a corrective factor or handicap should be considered in favor of elRubius when considering the date of publication of both videos: 21 December 2017 and 8 May 2018. As, in both cases, several months have elapsed since its release, there seems to be no balancing effect or change that elRubius would overcome the number of video views of the first.

A final combination of all the collected quantitative data is provided in Table 4.

Table 4. Total number of subscribers and video views per genre in the top 10 Spanish YouTubers (5 May 2018).

	Memes	**Children Videos/Videogames**	**Videogames**
	TheChacal547	Doggy Doggy Play Doh Cartoons	VEGETTA777
	Makiman131	Mejores juguetes	elRubiusOMG
		Mikecrack	Oxiris
		Las Ratitas	
		Doh Motion	
SUBSCRIBERS	8,452,689	20,258,331	51,818,288
VIDEO VIEWS	2,365,494,439	8,318,730,155	15,401,691,883

This table provides revealing data. Of the approximate total number of subscribers to successful Spanish YouTubers' channels (about 81 million) on the date of analysis, approximately 36% would be under eight years old (about 29 million) with genres focused on children's content, and the remaining 64% would also be focused on pseudo-childish content. From these data, I concluded that the average user of this kind of channel in Spain would be less than eight years old and consumes mainly children's content. If this relevant age category is not considered in terms of total numbers, the average Spanish subscriber would be older than eight years old and consumes content specifically related to videogames (aimed at them) and memes.

4. Discussion and Conclusions

In reference to my objectives proposed in this paper, I concluded that: (1) In terms of gender or/and sex visualization, most YouTubers are male. (2) The degree of originality can be considered as very low, due to both the uniformity of the content among the different channels and to the minimal variety of the narrative strategies and staging within each particular channel, which reminds us of primitive cinema. These are videos made with professional means of production, but whose creation tends to amateurism or, at least, to a certain immediacy. (3) To answer the question as to whether YouTubers' channels by themselves compose a totally new audio-visual genre, I think that these channels are a new audiovisual genre that, despite the minimal originality when compared with other YouTuber channels, display unique features, such as channels with polymediation, although these are not too developed.

To answer the question posed by McRobie [15], these YouTubers do not appear to have "a new radical voice". Instead, these channels resemble the Amazon-type monetization that is typical for YouTube content. However, these channels are also related to the monetization of self-centeredness or, as Duffy defined, to the mercantilization of a certain vocation related to the pregnant world of communication. This, when mixed with the different kinds of narcissism of YouTubers and the user themselves [3–7], exceeds what a Marxist critical analysis of mercantilist Neoliberalism could provide.

Burgess and Green [13], Jenkins [17], Sabich and Steinberg [18], and Lange [19] pointed out how YouTube is part of a participatory or connected culture—a community that, in most cases, is quite poor considering that it is mainly based on "likes" and "dislikes", and on a basic commentary chat structure below the video window. Polymediation would require a deepening in the philosophy of the concept, for example, with the possibility for the users to "comment" with their own produced videos, or editing the videos uploaded by each YouTuber. With even more open communication, all the possibilities of polymediation could be applied. The current structure of the Youtuber ecosystem reinforces the influence of the YouTuber and their success. However, I think that in the medium term, polymediation will be a major limitation of the creativity and evolution of this ecosystem based on the accentuated generational bias that requires a rethinking of the whole ecosystem.

My research has certain limitations, both at the quantitative and qualitative levels. Of the former, a limitation was caused by the data being gathered on a single day, though I was able to integrate a brief comparison with subsequent data nine months later (Figure 11). Even without this comparison, this quantitative level allowed me to observe a clear trend in the goal of classifying successful audiovisual genres. I provided a finding that may be significant, but needs to be tested in other research: The obvious user age bias that problematizes the future development of these YouTuber channels. Qualitative limitations are always inherent if simply compared with the quantitative methods, but the qualitative methods here were especially necessary given the youth of this phenomenon in which the data's historical series are limited. As such, qualitative data can contribute significantly to this field. Polymediation is speculative, but I think it can contribute to the understanding and future development of the YouTube phenomenon.

In summary, my analysis could have been more comprehensive if it had included a lengthened body of research, both temporarily extending the time slot as well as more nationalities. However, my goal was also to propose a method that could be applied by other researchers. I have proposed a straightforward method so the results can be replicated in other cultures.

To finish, the concept of polymediation can be related to the successful audiovisual subgenres in Spain that I deduced. These are based on content aimed at specific audiences and with an emphatic type of communication that is related to polymediation, as this is a type of communication with which it is possible to connect, to invent qualitative new content, or reinvent the type of contact between the YouTuber and the user on a daily basis. Polymediation is reinforced by the feeling of community and the verification of identities that these audiovisual genres imply, especially in children, but also in teenagers if video-games are considered.

The definition of polymediation also provides some interesting research questions, especially in relation to the new possibilities for both narrative and business. I am not referring only to something so direct as direct monetization—so common in economics studies on YouTubers—and their professional projects. Polymediation provides research avenues in many aspects, including even sociological research, considering Baumann's liquid modernity, such as when Calka sustains that polymediation shows how "the complex relationship between media, identity, and performance is necessarily in flux" [28] (pp. 27, 28). This flux that YouTubers are unconsciously building must be considered, although, given the style and content of the dominant genres in their channels, it is still an immature flow, but one that marks a clear path. If one agrees with Calka that our identities change with the changes in the technological landscape of the media (ibid.)—the continuous flow related to Baumann thought—one must consider the bias that mediates a large part of the adults in our society by specific YouTubers genres that indirectly and proportionally offer content that do not respond proportionally to the cultural richness of a culture that has been able to offer the most sophisticated communication network in history.

To the best of my knowledge, this is the first study in which polymediation was related to YouTube success. My results indicate that polymediation has not been fully developed in YouTube channels, a kind of audiovisual entertainment. I envision a difficulty and two possibilities. Firstly, according to the data I presented, this is a fairly mature market in which approximately the five top YouTubers have sufficient subscribers and views to live off the income and are able to set trends, so specificity is a difficulty for newcomers. As for the possibilities, both the YouTube platform and the analyzed channels are recent, and both have provided examples of creativity and flexibility since its creation, which are characteristics of polymediation. Seeking survival may produce radical changes in the medium term. Secondly, YouTube is the paradigm—although in its most basic expression—of polymediation. However, traditional on-line content platforms (OTT), such as Netflix or Amazon, are degrading the ecosystem of immediate consumption and in no entertainment area is YouTube the king. This can be expected to spur YouTube—and YouTubers themselves—to implement new polymediation features that would provide YouTube channels an advantage over OTTs. This advantage is yet to be seen, but the situation suggests that it will be along the lines of polymediation. When I was finishing this article, on 28 December 2018 Netflix had just released *Black Mirror: Bandersnatch*, the first interactive chapter of the series, in which the viewer makes decisions for the main character, being asked at various points to make a choice which affects the storyline [44]. I think that change will accelerate as the generational bias disappears, which is when the users of these channels aged. Considerably more work is needed to determine its further development.

More information on polymediation would help with the establishment of a greater degree of accuracy on this matter. My future lines of research will be developed along these lines, in trying to analyze how the possibilities offered by polymediation can be integrated into successful YouTube channels. I will analyze similar YouTubers' examples as proposed here, but from different cultures, such as the North American, Russian, or Chinese cultures. Later, I will compare the results to look for similarities and differences to verify to what extent the integration of polymediation can be generalized at the global level. My intent will be to propose a guide both methodological—for the analysis of the YouTuber phenomenon—and professional to provide a minimum guideline of success for future YouTubers, as well as a sufficient ethical guideline that is globally valid.

The aim of the present research was to examine the predominant audiovisual genres of the successful YouTube channels in Spain and their relationship with polymediation. This led me to a discussion the creation of the identity of their users. This was not the focus of this paper, but from a sociological point of view, for example, from Bauman [45], identity is created from the various alternative offers that are present in our reality (p. 16). It is nowadays accepted that texts, those that surround us and compose our daily life, build our consciousness, and the quality of these texts qualitatively influence our identities. "The media supply 'virtual [...] substitute' and 'imagined extra territoriality' to the multitude of people who are denied access to real life" (p. 97). Therefore, my analysis expands the field of study mapped here from the data collected, as hypothesized. I attempted to think about polymediation in YouTuber channels beyond the technical possibility, for example, analysing how it can influence the creation of mature identities that can face the challenges of our liquid society.

From a more philosophical viewpoint, Byung-Chul Han [46] examined this possibility when claiming that the Internet does not really assist human intercommunication, but enables contact with peers and distances strangers and those who are different. Pariser thinks that all this would narrow our horizon as "we are entangled in an endless loop of the self and, ultimately, lead us to a 'self-propaganda that indoctrinates us with our own notions'" [47]. A further comprehension of what polymediation could add might help to overcome this level of childish self-centeredness.

Funding: This research was funded by Ministerio de Economía, Industria y Competitividad [Ministry of Economy, Industry and Competitiveness], Ref. CSO2016-74977-R. "Análisis del fenómeno Youtubers en España: Una exploración para identificar los vectores de cambio del mercado audiovisual" ["Analysis of the YouTubers Phenomenon in Spain: An Exploration to Identify the Vectors of Change in the Audio-visual Market"], 2016/00171/010, Proyecto I+d Plan Nacional. Universidad Rey Juan Carlos.

Conflicts of Interest: The author declares no conflict of interest.

References

1. Roberts, C.; Muscarella, V. *OTT Overview*; Digital EMA (Entertainment Merchants Association): North Hollywood, CA, USA, 2015. p. 1. Available online: http://www.entmerch.org/digitalema/white-papers/defining-digital-distributi.pdf (accessed on 7 January 2019).
2. Torres, L. Aproximación a un modelo de representación virtual lúdico (MRVL). Virtual Self, narcisismo y ausencia de sentido. *Cuad. 56. Cuad.Cent. Estud. Dis. Com.* **2016**, [Approach to a Playful Virtual Representation Model (MRVL). Virtual Self, Narcissism and Lack of Meaning]. *56*, 227–250. Available online: https://www.academia.edu/11522141/Aproximación_a_un_modelo_de_representación_virtual_lúdico_MRVL_._Virtual_Self_narcisismo_y_ausencia_de_sentido (accessed on 5 December 2018).
3. Ksinan, A.J.; Vazsonyi, A.T. Narcissism, Internet, and Social Relations: A Study of Two Tales. *Personal. Individ. Differ.* **2016**, *94*, 118–123. [CrossRef]
4. In Levy, F. *Becoming a Star in the Youtube Revolution*; Alpha. A member of Penguin Group: London, UK, 2008.
5. Cocker, H.L.; Cronin, J. Charismatic authority and the YouTuber: Unpacking the new cults of personality. *Market. Theory* **2017**, 1–18. [CrossRef]
6. Ashman, R.; Patterson, A.; Brown, S. 'Don't Forget to Like, Share and Subscribe': Digital Autopreneurs in a Neoliberal World. *J. Bus. Res.* **2018**, *92*, 474–483. [CrossRef]
7. Lange, P.G. Videos of Affinity on YouTube. In *The YouTube Reader*; Snickars, P., Vonderau, P., Eds.; National Library of Sweden: Stockholm, Sweden, 2009; pp. 70–88.
8. Instituto Cervantes. El español: Una lengua viva. Informe 2017. Available online: https://cvc.cervantes.es/lengua/espanol_lengua_viva/pdf/espanol_lengua_viva_2017.pdf (accessed on 3 December 2018).
9. Lindley, C. Narrative, Game Play, and Alternative Time Structures for Virtual Environments. In *Technologies for Interactive Digital Storytelling and Entertainment: Proceedings of TIDSE 2004*; Göbel, S., Ed.; Springer: Darmstadt, Germany, 2004; pp. 183–194.
10. Berlant, L. *Cruel Optimism*; Duke University Press: London, UK, 2011. [CrossRef]

11. Hess, A. Resistance Up in Smoke: Analyzing the Limitations of Deliberation on YouTube. *Crit. Stud. Med. Commun.* **2009**, *26*, 411–434. [CrossRef]
12. Bell, E.J.; Owen, T.; Brown, P.D.; Hauka, C.; Rashidian, N. *The Platform Press: How Silicon Valley Reengineered Journalism*; Columbia Journalism School, Tow Center for Digital Journalism: New York, NY, USA, 2017; p. 50. [CrossRef]
13. Burguess, J.; Green, J. The Entrepreneurial Vlogger: Participatory Culture: Beyond the Professional-Amateur Divide. In *The YouTube Reader*; Snickars, P., Vonderau, P., Eds.; National Library of Sweden: Stockholm, Sweden, 2009; pp. 89–107.
14. Duffy, B.E. *(Not) Getting Paid to Do What You Love. Gender, Social Media, and Aspirational Work*; Yale University Press: New Haven, CT, USA; London, UK, 2017; p. XII, (Preface).
15. McRobie, A. *Be Creative: Making a Living in the New Culture Industries*; Polity: Cambridge, UK, 2016; pp. 3–16.
16. Burguess, J.; Green, J. *Youtube. Online Video and Participatory Culture*; Polity: Cambridge, UK, 2018; pp. vii, 5–6.
17. Jenkins, H. *Convergence Culture. Where Old and New Media Collide*; New York University Press: New York, NY, USA; London, UK, 2006; pp. 3–4.
18. Sabich, M.A.; Steinberg, L. Discursividad youtuber: Afecto, narrativas y estrategias de socialización en comunidades de Internet. *Mediterr. J. Commun.* **2017**, *8*, 171–188. [CrossRef]
19. Lange, P. Publicly Private and Privately Public: Social Networking on YouTube. *J. Comput.-Mediat. Commun.* **2007**, *13*, 361–380. [CrossRef]
20. Elorriaga, A.; Monge, S. The Professionalization of YouTubers: The Case of Verdeliss and the Brands. *Rev. Latina Comun. Soc.* **2018**, *73*, 37–54. [CrossRef]
21. Pérez-Torres, V.; Pastor-Ruiz, Y.; Abarrou-Ben-Boubaker, S. YouTubers Videos and the Construction of Adolescent Identity. *Comunicar* **2018**, *55*, 61–70. [CrossRef]
22. Ramos-Serrano, M.; Herrero-Diz, P. Unboxing and Brands: Youtubers Phenomenon through the Case Study of EvanTubeHD. *Prisma Soc.* **2016**, *1*, 90–130.
23. Scolari, C.A.; Fraticelli, D. The case of the top Spanish YouTubers Emerging Media Subjects and Discourse Practices in the New Media Ecology. *Convergence Int. J. Res. New Media Technol.* **2017**, 1–20. [CrossRef]
24. Scolari, C.A. The Grammar of Hypertelevision. An Identikit of the Convergence Age Television (Or How Television is Simulating New Interactive Media). *J. Vis. Lit.* **2009**, *28*, 28–49. [CrossRef]
25. Berzosa, M.I. *Youtubers y otras especies. El fenómeno que ha cambiado la manera de entender los contenidos audiovisuales*; Ariel, Fundación Telefónica: Madrid, Spain, 2017; p. 11.
26. Available online: https://socialblade.com/youtube/help/what-is-sbrank-all-about (accessed on 31 January 2019).
27. Madianou, M.; Miller, D. Polymedia: Towards a New Theory of Digital Media in Interpersonal Communication. *Int. J. Cult. Stud.* **2012**, *16*, 169–187. [CrossRef]
28. Calka, M. Polymediation. The Relationship between Self and Media. In *Beyond New Media: Discourse and Critique in a Polymediated Age*; Herbig, A., Herrmann, A.F., Tyma, A.W., Calka, M., Denker, K.J., Dunn, R.A., Henderson, C., Manning, J., Stern, D.M., Willits, M.D.D., Eds.; Lexington Books: Lanham, MD, USA, 2015; pp. 15–30.
29. Wall, D. Identity Related Crime in the UK. London: Government Office for Science. In *Foresight Future Identities. Final Project Report*; The Government Office for Science: London, UK, 2013; p. 25. Available online: http://tedcantle.co.uk/wp-content/uploads/2013/03/074-Foresight-Future-Identities-2013-Report-by-the-Government-Office-for-Science1.pdf (accessed on 16 December 2018).
30. Baym, K. *Personal Connections un the Digital Age*, 2nd ed.; Polity: Cambridge, UK, 2015; pp. 6–12.
31. Couldry, N. Digital Storytelling, Media Research and Democracy: Conceptual Choices and Alternative Futures. In *Digital Storytelling, Mediatized Stories: Self-Representations in New Media. Digital Formations (52)*; Lundby, K., Ed.; Peter Lang Publishing, Inc.: New York, NY, USA, 2008; pp. 41–60.
32. Livingstone, S. On the mediation of everything: ICA presidential address 2008. *J. Commun.* **2008**, *59*, 1–18. [CrossRef]
33. Couldry, N. *Media, Society, World: Social Theory and Digital Media Practice*; Polity: Cambridge, UK, 2012.
34. Hepp, A. Transculturality as a Perspective: Researching Media Cultures Comparatively. *Forum Qual. Sozialforschung* **2009**, *10*, 26.
35. Hjarvard, S. Changing Media, Changing Language: The Mediatization of Society and the Spread of English and Medialects'. In Proceedings of the 57th ICA Conference, San Francisco, CA, USA, 23–28 May 2007.
36. Friedman, T.L. *The World is Flat. A Brief History of the Twenty-First Century*; Picador: New York, NY, USA, 2005.

37. TheChacal547. Available online: https://www.youtube.com/user/thechacal547 (accessed on 17 December 2018).
38. elRubius. Available online: https://www.youtube.com/channel/UCXazgXDIYyWH-yXLAkcrFxw (accessed on 18 December 2018).
39. VEGETTA777. Available online: https://www.youtube.com/user/vegetta777 (accessed on 18 December 2018).
40. Mejores Juguetes. Available online: https://www.youtube.com/user/MejoresJuguetes (accessed on 18 December 2018).
41. Martín Ruiz, J.M. Los factores definitorios de los grandes grupos de edad de la población: Tipos, subgrupos y umbrales. Scripta Nova 2005, IX, 190. Available online: http://www.ub.edu/geocrit/sn/sn-190.htm (accessed on 28 December 2018).
42. As of December 28, 2018. Available online: https://www.youtube.com/watch?v=-AW1WpH8VPQ (accessed on 28 December 2018).
43. 13,093,648 views on December 29, 2018. Available online: https://www.youtube.com/watch?v=fTc8bwoSv4M&t=2s (accessed on 29 December 2018).
44. Available online: https://www.netflix.com (accessed on 30 January 2018).
45. Bauman, Z. *Identity. Conversations with Benedetti Vecchi*; Polity Press: Cambridge, UK, 2004.
46. Han, B. *La expulsión de lo distinto [Die Austreibung des Anderen, 2016]*; Herder: Barcelona, Spain, 2017; Volumen 5.11. Available online: http://www.emanantial.com.ar/archivos/fragmentos/HanLEDFragmentopdf (accessed on 1 February 2019).
47. Pariser, E. *Filter Bubble. Wie wir im Internet Entmündigt Werden*; Carl Hanser: Munich, Germany, 2012; p. 22.

© 2019 by the author. Licensee MDPI, Basel, Switzerland. This article is an open access article distributed under the terms and conditions of the Creative Commons Attribution (CC BY) license (http://creativecommons.org/licenses/by/4.0/).

 *future internet*

Review

Open Data for Open Innovation: An Analysis of Literature Characteristics

Diego Corrales-Garay [†], Eva-María Mora-Valentín [*,†] and Marta Ortiz-de-Urbina-Criado [†]

Facultad de Ciencias Jurídicas y Sociales, Universidad Rey Juan Carlos, Paseo de los Artilleros, s/n, 28032 Madrid, Spain; diego.corrales@urjc.es (D.C.-G.); marta.ortizdeurbina@urjc.es (M.O.-d.-U.-C.)
* Correspondence: evamaria.mora@urjc.es; Tel.: +34-91-495-9256
† These authors contributed equally to this work.

Received: 19 February 2019; Accepted: 20 March 2019; Published: 24 March 2019

Abstract: In this paper, we review some characteristics of the literature that studies the uses and applications of open data for open innovation. Three research questions are proposed about both topics: (1) What journals, conferences and authors have published papers about the use of open data for open innovation? (2) What knowledge areas have been analysed in research on open data for open innovation? and (3) What are the methodological characteristics of the papers on open data for open innovation? To answer the first question, we use a descriptive analysis to identify the relevant journals and authors. To address the second question, we identify the knowledge areas of the studies about open data for open innovation. Finally, we analyse the methodological characteristics of the literature (type of study, analytical techniques, sources of information and geographical area). Our results show that the applications of open data for open innovation are interesting but their multidisciplinary nature makes the context complex and diverse, opening up many future avenues for research. To develop a future research agenda, we propose a theoretical model and some research questions to analyse the open data impact process for open innovation.

Keywords: open data; open innovation; literature review; authors; journals; knowledge areas; methodological characteristics

1. Introduction

Since the beginning of the 2000s, the use of the term "open" has increased exponentially [1], giving rise to concepts such as open data, open innovation, open medical records system, open science, open knowledge, and open education, among others.

In 2003, Chesbrough proposed a new paradigm of the innovation [2,3]. For this author, open innovation constitutes a model where firms use both external and internal resources and commercialize both external and internal ideas/technologies [2]. Open innovation is defined as "The use of purposive inflows and outflows of knowledge to accelerate internal innovation, and expand the markets for external use of innovation, respectively. Open innovation is a paradigm that assumes that firms can and should use external ideas as well as internal ideas, and internal and external paths to market, as the firms look to advance their technology" [4] (p. 1). In that sense, open data is an external source that can be used for generating open innovation, and open innovations can create open data.

The open data concept alludes to "data that anyone can access, use, and share. Governments, businesses and individuals can use open data to bring about social, economic, and environmental benefits" [5]. Its annual economic impact is important to note: Open data potentially generate 900 billion dollars in the global economy [6], with a European Union market share increase of 36.9% between 2016 and 2020 [7]. Open data offer the potential for reuse, which produces new, innovative services for citizens and society in general [8,9]. Likewise, open data initiatives have an impact on aspects such as citizen engagement, transparency and innovation in the public sector [10].

We see then that open data can be a source to innovate. Some authors highlight that it is interesting to understand, in the context of open data and smart cities, how data-driven innovation is performed and its creation of social and economic value for the society [9,11]. Considering the interest of studying innovation in the context of open data and the importance of the openness phenomenon, we examine the possibility of using open data for open innovation. In that sense, we have searched articles that offer state-of-the-art ideas on that theme but have not found literature reviews that join open data and open innovation. Due to this, we have searched literature reviews of each theme to look for interest to study the combination of those two terms. We have found literature reviews about open data using different methodologies and temporal scopes [12–15]. Other studies analyse the literature on open innovation, combining several methodologies and temporal scopes, with 2017 being the last year analysed in the most current articles [16–25]. Finally, we have found that some of these studies have identified interest in the relationship between the terms "open data" and "open innovation" [12,14,17].

In that context, open data offers access to internal and external data that come from, mainly, public organisations. Governments and public agencies are liberating their data and they want open data to be used to solve problems and to create and improve products and services. However, access to open data in itself does not produce innovation [26]. New services, created by open data, mainly software applications, can be produced using a process known as open innovation, defined as "the opening of the innovation process to knowledge from outside the innovating organisation" [27] (p. 2), in which diverse agents such as citizens, companies, public entities, or academia collaborate to co-create these new services [28]. Thus, it is necessary to know how to implement open innovation using open data. A first stage to develop that idea is to review the previous literature.

In this paper, we have analysed the characteristics of the previous literature that has related open data with open innovation. We propose three research questions: (1) What journals, conferences and authors have published papers about the use of open data for open innovation? (2) What knowledge areas have been analysed in research on open data for open innovation? and (3) What are the methodological characteristics of the papers on open data for open innovation? To answer the first question, we use a descriptive analysis to identify the relevant journals and authors. To address the second question, we identify the knowledge areas of the studies about open data for open innovation. Finally, we analyse the methodological characteristics of the literature (type of study, analytical techniques, sources of information and geographical area). After answering these three questions, we will be better able to (a) identify who is who in that research line; (b) show the opportunities to implement open innovation to the agents of the open data ecosystem and (c) orient the new research about the use of open data for open innovation

2. Methods Search Protocol

The Web of Science (WoS) and Scopus databases were used to perform the literature review, since they are the most relevant databases in academia. While WoS included 20,000 indexed journals, Scopus included 21,950 [29].

The search protocol used is:

- Search date: 8 March 2019.
- Search resources: WoS and Scopus databases.
- Data range inclusive all years to 2018.
- Documents searched by "Theme" (WoS) or "Article title, Abstract, Keywords" (Scopus).
- Inclusion criteria: articles, conference papers and all access type.
- Search terms used: "open data" OR open-data AND "open innovation" OR open-innovation.
- Number of documents without filtered: 34 (WoS) and 56 (Scopus).
- Filtered process: exclude duplicates and the conference reviews that do not identify the authors.
- Final number of documents: 55.

3. Results

3.1. Descriptive Analysis

Figure 1 presents the number of documents per year for the combination of the two topics studied. The first publications are from 2012 (4), and a certain growth can be seen from 2014 to 2017, with the highest number of documents appearing in 2015 (13) and 2017 (13).

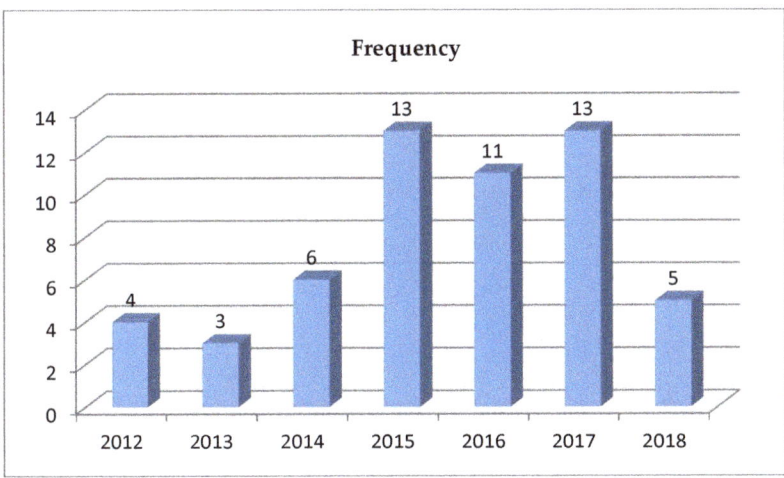

Figure 1. Number of documents per year.

Table 1 shows the details of the documents identified in our analysis: authors, year of publication, title, citations in WoS, and Scopus and type of paper (articles: 28; conference papers: 27).

Table 1. Document analysis: Author/s, year/title/number of citations (WoS and Scopus).

Author/s, Year	Title	Citations	
		WoS	Scopus
Bonazzi & Liu, 2015 [30] (CP)	Two Birds with One Stone. An Economically Viable Solution for Linked Open Data Platforms	-	0
Boubin, 2017 [31] (CP)	Importance of Open Innovation Mode for Start-Up Projects	0	-
Cândido, Vianna, Gauthier, Aradas & Koslovsky, 2015 [32] (A)	Proposta de Modelo para Avaliação e Supervisão de Gestão da Inovação Tecnológica em Pequenas e Médias Organizações	-	0
Chan, 2013 [33] (CP)	From Open Data to Open Innovation Strategies: Creating e-Services Using Open Government Data	20	45
Chatfield & Reddick, 2017 [34] (A)	A Longitudinal Cross-Sector Analysis of Open Data Portal Service Capability: The Case of Australian Local Governments	7	11
Conradie, Mulder & Choenni, 2012 [28] (CP)	Rotterdam Open Data: Exploring the Release of Public Sector Information through Co-Creation	-	10
Dardier, 2018 [35] (CP)	Open Access to Digital Information at the University for Applied Sciences and Arts Western Switzerland	-	0

Table 1. Cont.

Author/s, Year	Title	Citations	
		WoS	Scopus
De Freitas & Dacorso, 2014 [36] (A)	Inovação Aberta na Gestão Pública: Análise do Plano de Ação Brasileiro para a Open Government Partnership	-	1
Del Frate, Mothe, Barbier, Becker, Olszewski & Soudris, 2017 [37] (CP)	FabSpace 2.0: The Open-Innovation Network for Geodata-Driven Innovation	0	2
Emaldi, Aguilera, López-de-Ipiña & Pérez-Velasco, 2017 [38] (A)	Towards Citizen Co-Created Public Service Apps	0	0
Fortunato, Gorgoglione, Messeni Petruzzelli & Panniello, 2017 [39] (A)	Leveraging Big Data for Sustaining Open Innovation: The Case of Social TV	3	4
Gagliardi, Schina, Sarcinella, Mangialardi, Niglia & Corallo, 2017 [40] (A)	Information and Communication Technologies and Public Participation: Interactive Maps and Value Added for Citizens	6	13
Gold, 2016 [41] (A)	Accelerating Translational Research through Open Science: The Neuro Experiment	2	-
Ham, Lee, Kim & Choi, 2015 [42] (CP)	Open Innovation Maturity Model for the Government: An Open System Perspective	-	4
Hellberg & Hedström, 2015 [43] (A)	The Story of the Sixth Myth of Open Data and Open Government	13	20
Herala, Vanhala, Porras & Kärri, 2016 [12] (CP)	Experiences about Opening Data in Private Sector: A Systematic Literature Review	2	-
Hjalmarsson, Johannesson, Juell-Skielse & Rudmark, 2014 [44] (CP)	Beyond Innovation Contests: A Framework of Barriers to Open Innovation of Digital Services	-	11
Hoel, 2014 [45] (CP)	Standards as Enablers for Innovation in Education—The Breakdown of European Pre-Standardisation	0	1
Huber, Wainwright & Rentocchini, 2018 [46] (A)	Open Data for Open Innovation: Managing Absorptive Capacity in SMEs	-	0
Jaakola, Kekkonen, Lahti & Manninen, 2015 [47] (A)	Open Data, Open Cities: Experiences from the Helsinki Metropolitan Area. Case Helsinki Region Infoshare www.hri.fi	-	8
Jaakkola, Mäkinen, Henno & Mäkelä, 2014 [48] (CP)	Open^n	2	3
Juell-Skielse, Hjalmarsson, Juell-Skielse, Johannesson & Rudmark, 2014 [49] (A)	Contests as Innovation Intermediaries in Open Data Markets	-	8
Kassen, 2017 [10] (A)	Open Data in Kazakhstan: Incentives, Implementation and Challenges	4	10
Katsonis & Botros, 2015 [50] (A)	Digital Government: A Primer and Professional Perspectives	0	-
Kauppinen, 2015 [51] (CP)	Enhancing Public e-Service Development with Citizens' Self-Organized Collaboration	9	11
Kauppinen, Luojus & Lahti, 2016 [52] (CP)	Involving Citizens in Open Innovation Process by Means of Gamification: The Case of WeLive	2	6
Kuhlman, Ramamurthy, Sattigeri, Lozano, Cao, Reddy, Mojsilovic & Varshney, 2017 [53] (A)	How to Foster Innovation: A Data-Driven Approach to Measuring Economic Competitiveness	1	1
Lee, Ham & Choi, 2016 [54] (CP)	Effect of Government Data Openness on a Knowledge-Based Economy	2	3
Lin, 2015 [55] (A)	Open Data and Co-Production of Public Value of BBC Backstage	3	4
Lin, Wang & Yang, 2012 [56] (A)	TOUCH Doctor—A Nutrition Control Service System Developed under Living Lab Methodology	-	1
Lin, Wang & Yang, 2013 [57] (CP)	Developed Smart Nutrient Services with Living Lab Methodology	0	0
López de Ipiña, Emaldi, Aguilera & Pérez Velasco, 2016 [58] (CP)	Towards Citizen Co-Created Public Service Apps	0	3

Table 1. Cont.

Author/s, Year	Title	Citations WoS	Citations Scopus
Luojus, Kauppinen, Lahti & Tahtinen, 2017 [59] (CP)	Forming Multidisciplinary Master's Degree Student Teams by Means of Gamification Case: The WeLive Design Game	0	-
Nikiforov & Singireja, 2016 [60] (CP)	Open Data and Crowdsourcing Perspectives for Smart City in the United States and Russia	-	0
Noda, Duan, Fukushiro, Yoshida & Coughlan, 2017 [61] (CP)	The Classification, Challenge and Potential of Business Models by Using Open Data	-	1
Noda, Honda, Yoshida & Coughlan, 2016 [62] (CP)	Review of Estimation Method of Economic Effects Created by Using Open Data	-	1
Owens, 2016 [63] (A)	Curating in the Open: A Case for Iteratively and Openly Publishing Curatorial Research on the Web	0	1
Perkmann & Schildt, 2015 [64] (A)	Open Data Partnerships between Firms and Universities: The Role of Boundary Organizations	30	37
Piedra, Chicaiza, Lopez-Vargas & Caro, 2016 [65] (CP)	Guidelines to Producing Structured Interoperable Data from Open Access Repositories	0	11
Reisdorf, Chhugani, Sanseau & Agarwal, 2017 [66] (A)	Harnessing Public Domain Data to Discover and Validate Therapeutic Targets	1	-
Saxena, 2018 [67] (A)	Asymmetric Open Government Data (OGD) Framework in India	0	-
Shiramatsu, Tossavainen, Ozono & Shintani, 2015 [68] (CP)	Towards Continuous Collaboration on Civic Tech Projects: Use Cases of a Goal Sharing System Based on Linked Open Data	3	6
Smith & Sandberg, 2018 [69] (A)	Barriers to Innovating with Open Government Data: Exploring Experiences across Service Phases and User Types	0	0
Smith & Seward, 2017 [1] (A)	Openness as Social Praxis	-	6
Stephenson, Di Lorenzo & Aonghusa, 2012 [70] (CP)	Open Innovation Portal: A Collaborative Platform for Open City Data Sharing	-	4
Susha, Grönlund & Janssen, 2015 [71] (A)	Driving Factors of Service Innovation Using Open Government Data: An Exploratory Study of Entrepreneurs in Two Countries	-	11
Tossavainen, Shiramatsu, Ozono & Shintani, 2014 [72] (CP)	Implementing a System Enabling Open Innovation by Sharing Public Goals Based on Linked Open Data	-	2
Tossavainen, Shiramatsu, Ozono & Shintani, 2016 [73] (A)	A Linked Open Data Based System Utilizing Structured Open Innovation Process for Addressing Collaboratively Public Concerns in Regional Societies	2	2
Tucci, Viscusi & Gautschi, 2018 [74] (A)	Translating Science into Business Innovation: The Case of Open Food and Nutrition Data	0	-
Väyrynen, Helander & Vasell, 2017 [75] (A)	Knowledge Management for Open Innovation: Comparing Research Results between SMEs and Large Companies	1	1
Viseur, 2015 [76] (CP)	Open Science: Practical Issues in Open Research Data	-	1
Wells, Willis, Burrows & Van Huijsduijnen, 2016 [77] (A)	Open Data in Drug Discovery and Development: Lessons from Malaria	9	14
Yang & Kanhanhalli, 2013 [78] (CP)	Innovation in Government Services: The Case of Open Data	-	26
Zdrazil, Blomberg & Ecker, 2012 [79] (A)	Taking Open Innovation to the Molecular Level—Strengths and Limitations	5	7
Zimmermann & Pucihar, 2015 [27] (CP)	Open Innovation, Open Data and New Business Models	1	1

A: Article; CP: Conference paper.

3.1.1. Journals and Conferences

Tables 2–4 present the analysis of the documents according to type: articles or conference papers. Regarding articles (Tables 2 and 3), the "Information Polity" and "Government Information Quarterly" journals stand out with three and two articles, respectively. Regarding conference papers (Table 4), the book series "Lectures Notes in Computer Science" stands out with three documents. The other journals and sources only have one document each.

Table 2. Articles: journal/ranking and category JCR.

Journal	Ranking and Category JCR	Articles
Information Polity	NA	3
Government Information Quarterly	Q1 (Information Science & Library Science—SSCI)	2
IBM Journal of Research and Development	Q3 (Computer Science, Hardware & Architecture—SCIE), Q4 (Computer Science, Information Systems—SCIE), Q3 (Computer Science, Software Engineering—SCIE), Q3 (Computer Science, Theory & Methods—SCIE)	1
Information Systems Management	Q3 (Computer Science, Information Systems—SCIE)	1
Sensors	Q2 (Chemistry, Analytical—SCIE), Q3 (Electrochemistry—SCIE), Q2 (Instruments & Instrumentation—SCIE)	1
International Journal of Innovation Management	NA	1
First Monday	NA	1
Information Technology and People	Q2 (Information Science & Library Science—SSCI)	1
Curator: The Museum Journal	NA	1
Nature Reviews Drug Discovery	Q1 (Biotechnology & Applied Microbiology—SCIE), Q1 (Pharmacology & Pharmacy)	1
Applied Intelligence	Q2 (Computer Science, Artificial Intelligence)	1
Research Policy	Q1 (Management—SSCI), Q1 (Planning & Development—SSCI)	1
International Journal of Digital Television	NA	1
Transforming Government: People, Process and Policy	NA	1
Statistical Journal of the IAOS	NA	1
Australian Journal of Public Administration	Q3 (Public Administration—SSCI)	1
Espacios	NA	1
Revista de Administração Pública	NA	1
Molecular Informatics	Q3 (Chemistry, Medicinal—SCIE), Q3 (Computer Science, Interdisciplinary Applications—SCIE), Q2 (Mathematical & Computational Biology—SCIE)	1
International Journal of Automation and Smart Technology	NA	1
R and D Management	Q3 (Business—SSCI), Q3 (Management—SSCI)	1
Frontiers in Nutrition	NA	1
Digital Policy Regulation and Governance	NA	1
Expert Opinion on Drug Discovery	Q1 (Pharmacology & Pharmacy—SCIE)	1
PLOS Biology	Q1 (Biochemistry & Molecular Biology—SCIE), Q1 (Biology—SCIE)	1

Note: NA: not available.

Table 3. Articles: journal/ranking, subject area and category SJR.

Journal	Ranking, Subject Area and Category SJR	Articles
Information Polity	Q2 (Computer Science—Information System), Q2 (Social Sciences—Communication), Q2 (Social Sciences—Geography, Planning and Development), Q2 (Social Sciences—Public Administration), Q2 (Social Sciences—Sociology and Political Science), Q1 (Social Sciences—E-learning)	3
Government Information Quarterly	Q1 (Social Sciences—Law), Q1 (Social Sciences—Library and Information Sciences), Q1 (Social Sciences—Sociology and Political Science)	2
IBM Journal of Research and Development	Q2 (Computer Science—Computer Science (miscellaneous))	1
Information Systems Management	Q2 (Computer Science—Computer Science Applications), Q2 (Computer Science—Information Systems), Q1 (Social Sciences—Library and Information Sciences)	1
Sensors	Q3 (Biochemistry, Genetics and Molecular Biology—Biochemistry), Q2 (Chemistry—Analytical Chemistry), Q2 (Engineering—Electrical and Electronic Engineering), Q2 (Medicine—Medicine (miscellaneous)), Q2 (Physics and Astronomy—Atomic and Molecular Physics, and Optics Instrumentation)	1
International Journal of Innovation Management	Q2 (Business, Management and Accounting—Business and International Management), Q3 (Business, Management and Accounting—Management of Technology and Innovation), Q2 (Business, Management and Accounting—Strategy and Management)	1
First Monday	Q1 (Computer Science—Computer Networks and Communications), Q2 (Computer Science—Human-Computer Interaction), Q1 (Social Sciences—Law)	1
Information Technology and People	Q2 (Computer Science—Computer Science Applications), Q1 (Computer Science—Information Systems), Q1 (Social Sciences—Library and Information Sciences)	1
Curator: The Museum Journal	Q2 (Arts and Humanities—Conservation), Q2 (Arts and Humanities—Museology)	1
Nature Reviews Drug Discovery	Q1 (Medicine—Medicine (miscellaneous)), Q1 (Pharmacology, Toxicology and Pharmaceutics—Drug Discovery), Q1 (Pharmacology, Toxicology and Pharmaceutics—Pharmacology)	1
Applied Intelligence	Q2 (Computer Science—Artificial Intelligence)	1
Research Policy	Q1 (Business, Management and Accounting—Management of Technology and Innovation), Q1 (Business, Management and Accounting—Strategy and Management), Q1 (Decision Sciences—Management Science and Operations Research), Q1 (Engineering—Engineering (miscellaneous))	1

Table 3. Cont.

Journal	Ranking, Subject Area and Category SJR	Articles
International Journal of Digital Television	Q3 (Engineering—Media Technology), Q4 (Social Sciences—Communication), Q4 (Social Sciences—Sociology and Political Science)	1
Transforming Government: People, Process and Policy	Q2 (Computer Science—Computer Science Applications), Q2 (Decision Sciences—Information Systems and Management), Q2 (Social Sciences—E-learning), Q2 (Social Sciences—Public Administration)	1
Statistical Journal of the IAOS	Q2 (Business, Management and Accounting—Management Information Systems), Q3 (Decision Sciences—Statistics, Probability and Uncertainty), Q3 (Economics, Econometrics and Finance—Economics and Econometrics)	1
Australian Journal of Public Administration	Q2 (Social Sciences—Public Administration), Q2 (Social Sciences—Sociology and Political Science)	1
Espacios	Q3 (Business Management and Accounting—Business and International Management), Q4 (Business Management and Accounting—Management of Technology and Innovation), Q4 (Decision Sciences—Management Science and Operations Research)	1
Revista de Administração Pública	Q3 (Social Sciences—Public Administration)	1
Molecular Informatics	Q3 (Biochemistry, Genetics and Molecular Biology—Molecular Medicine), Q4 (Biochemistry, Genetics and Molecular Biology—Structural Biology), Q2 (Chemistry—Organic Chemistry), Q2 (Computer Science—Computer Science Applications), Q2 (Pharmacology, Toxicology and Pharmaceutics—Drug Discovery)	1
International Journal of Automation and Smart Technology	Q4 (Computer Science—Artificial Intelligence), Q4 (Computer Science—Hardware and Architecture), Q4 (Computer Science—Human-Computer Interaction), Q4 (Computer Science—Signal Processing), Q4 (Engineering—Control and Systems Engineering), Q4 (Engineering—Electrical and Electronic Engineering)	1
R and D Management	Q1 (Business, Management and Accounting—Business and International Management), Q1 (Business, Management and Accounting—Business, Management and Accounting (miscellaneous)), Q2 (Business, Management and Accounting—Management of Technology and Innovation), Q1 (Business, Management and Accounting—Strategy and Management)	1
Frontiers in Nutrition	NA	1
Digital Policy Regulation and Governance	Q2 (Business, Management and Accounting—Management Information Systems), Q3 (Business, Management and Accounting—Management of Technology and Innovation), Q2 (Computer Science—Computer Networks and Communications), Q3 (Computer Science—Information Systems), Q2 (Decision Sciences—Information Systems and Management)	1

Table 3. Cont.

Journal	Ranking, Subject Area and Category SJR	Articles
Expert Opinion on Drug Discovery	Q1 (Pharmacology, Toxicology and Pharmaceutics—Drug Discovery)	1
PLOS Biology	Q1 (Agricultural and Biological Sciences—Agricultural and Biological Sciences (miscellaneous)), Q1 (Biochemistry, Genetics and Molecular Biology—Biochemistry, Genetics and Molecular Biology (miscellaneous)), Q1 (Immunology and Microbiology—Immunology and Microbiology (miscellaneous)), Q1 (Neuroscience—Neuroscience (miscellaneous))	1

Note: NA: not available.

Table 4. Conference papers: source/ranking, subject area and category SJR *.

Source	Ranking, Subject Area and Category SJR	Conference Papers
Lecture Notes in Computer Science	Q2 (Computer Science—Computer Science (miscellaneous)), Q3 (Mathematics—Theoretical Computer Science)	3
37th Annual IEEE International Geoscience and Remote Sensing Symposium, IGARSS 2017	(Computer Science—Computer Science Applications), (Earth and Planetary Sciences—Earth and Planetary Sciences (miscellaneous))	1
13th International Symposium on Open Collaboration, OpenSym 2017	NA	1
46th Annual Frontiers in Education Conference, FIE 2016	(Computer Science—Computer Science Applications), (Computer Science—Software), (Social Sciences—Education)	1
3rd International Conference on Electronic Governance and Open Society: Challenges in Eurasia, EGOSE 2016	NA	1
9th Nordic Conference on Human-Computer Interaction, NordiCHI 2016	NA	1
12th International Symposium on Open Collaboration, OpenSym 2016	(Computer Science—Computer Science Applications), (Computer Science—Information Systems), (Computer Science—Software)	1
4th International Conference on Information Technology and Quantitative Management, ITQM 2016	NA	1
23rd Interdisciplinary Information Management Talks: Information Technology and Society—Interaction and Interdependence, IDIMT 2015	(Engineering—Control and System Engineering)	1
28th Bled eConference: #eWellbeing	(Computer Science—Computer Networks and Communications), (Computer Science—Computer Science Applications), (Computer Science—Information Systems), (Social Sciences—Education)	1
2015 International Conference on Information Systems: Exploring the Information Frontier, ICIS 2015	(Computer Science—Computer Networks and Communications), (Computer Science—Signal Processing), (Physics and Astronomy—Instrumentation)	1
4th International Conference on Data Management Technologies and Applications, DATA 2015	(Computer Science—Computer Science (miscellaneous))	1

Table 4. Cont.

Source	Ranking, Subject Area and Category SJR	Conference Papers
22nd European Conference on Information Systems, ECIS 2014	(Computer Science—Information Systems)	1
2014 37th International Convention on Information and Communication Technology, Electronics and Microelectronics, MIPRO 2014	(Computer Science—Computer Networks and Communications), (Engineering—Electrical and Electronic Engineering)	1
2014 6th ITU Kaleidoscope Academic Conference: Living in a Converged World—Impossible Without Standards? K 2014	(Computer Science—Computer Networks and Communications), (Social Sciences—E-learning)	1
1st International Conference on Orange Technologies, ICOT 2013	(Computer Science—Computer Networks and Communications)	1
46th Annual Hawaii International Conference on System Sciences, HICSS 2013	NA	1
2012 18th International Conference on Engineering, Technology and Innovation, ICE 2012	(Engineering—Engineering (miscellaneous)), (Engineering—Mechanics of Materials), (Mathematics—Computational Mathematics)	1
2012 IEEE International Conference on Pervasive Computing and Communications Workshops, PERCOM Workshops 2012	(Computer Science—Computer Networks and Communications), (Computer Science—Computer Science Applications)	1
IFIP Advances in Information and Communication Technology	Q3 (Computer Science—Computer Networks and Communications), Q4 (Computer Science—Information Systems), Q3 (Decision Sciences—Information Systems and Management)	1
1st International Conference on Digital Tools and Uses Congress, DTUC 2018	NA	1
Proceedings of the International Scientific Conference of Business Economics, Management and Marketing (ISCOBEMM 2017)	NA	1
10th International Conference of Education, Research and Innovation (ICERI 2017)	NA	1
Proceedings of the 2016 SAI Computing Conference (SAI)	(Computer Science—Computer Networks and Communications), (Computer Science—Computer Science Applications), (Engineering—Electrical and Electronic Engineering)	1
2015 SSR International Conference on Social Sciences and Information (SSR-SSI 2015)	NA	1

NA: not available. * Note: Information about conference papers ranking and categories JCR is not available.

We have analysed the different subject areas and categories of the Journal Citation Report (JCR) and Scimago Journal and Country Rank (SJR) (Tables 2–4). Most indicate a link with knowledge areas such as Information Technology and Computer Science and its offshoots. A review of the Computer Science subject area indicates the prevalence of the Computer Science Applications, Computer Networks, and Communication and Information Systems categories. Also prevalent are knowledge areas such as Public Administration and Government within the Social Sciences subject area, displaying a significant variety of associated categories: Sociology and Political Science, and Library and Information Sciences stand out, among others. Furthermore, knowledge areas such as Systems Engineering, Electronic Engineering or Electrical Engineering, among others (included in the Engineering subject area), have a significant presence. The Technology and Innovation Management knowledge area also appears, mainly linked with the subject areas of Business, Management and Accounting, and Decision Sciences. Medicine, Molecular Medicine, Pharmacology, and Chemoinformatics have a minor presence. Finally, we must mention the knowledge area of Museology, under the subject area of Arts & Humanities. When analysing the journals ranked by JCR, eight are in the first or second quartile and by SJR, 20 are in the first or second quartile for the last available year (2017).

3.1.2. Authors

Table 5 presents the most productive authors by affiliation and knowledge area. Several authors from the Nagoya Institute of Technology's Graduate School of Engineering (Nagoya, Japan) stand out with three publications each in the knowledge area of Computer Science: Tossavainen, Shiramatsu, Ozono and Shintani. Their publications focus on the use of web applications to promote collaboration between different interest groups (individuals or organisations) for the purpose of solving public and social problems [68,72,73].

Table 5. Top authors (affiliation and knowledge area).

Author	Affiliation	Knowledge Area	Documents
Tossavainen, T.	Graduate School of Engineering, Nagoya Institute of Technology, Nagoya, Japan/School of Science, Aalto University, Espoo, Finland	Computer Science/Physical Engineering/Acoustical	3
Shiramatsu, S.	Graduate School of Engineering, Nagoya Institute of Technology, Nagoya, Japan	Computer Science	3
Ozono, T.	Graduate School of Engineering, Nagoya Institute of Technology, Nagoya, Japan	Computer Science	3
Shintani, T.	Graduate School of Engineering, Nagoya Institute of Technology, Nagoya, Japan	Computer Science	3
Kauppinen, S.	Laurea University of Applied Sciences, Vantaa, Finland	Service Innovation and Design/Information Sciences/Computer Science	3
Noda, T.	Shimane University, Matsue City, Japan	Economics/Political Science	2
Yoshida, A.	Jawaharlal Nehru University, New Delhi, India	Economics/Computer Science	2
Coughlan, S.	Opendawn, Takamatsu-Shi, Japan	Economics	2
Emaldi, M.	DeustoTech—Deusto Foundation, University of Deusto, Bilbao, Spain	Computer Science	2
Aguilera, U.	DeustoTech—Deusto Foundation, University of Deusto, Bilbao, Spain	Computer Science	2
Pérez-Velasco, J.	Tecnalia, eServices, Madrid, Spain	Information and Communication Technology	2
Lee, J.N.	Korea University Business School, Seoul, Republic of Korea	Economics/Information Technology	2

Table 5. Cont.

Author	Affiliation	Knowledge Area	Documents
Ham, J.	Korea University Business School, Seoul, Republic of Korea	Hotel and Tourism Management	2
Choi, B.	Kookmin University, Seoul, Republic of Korea	Economics/Information Technology	2
Juell-Skielse, G.	Stockholm University, Stockholm, Sweden	Information Technology	2
Hjalmarsson, A.	Swedish ICT Viktoria and University of Borås, Gothenburg, Sweden	Information Technology/Sustainable Transportation	2
Johannesson, P.	Stockholm University, Stockholm, Sweden	Computer Science	2
Rudmark, D.	Swedish ICT Viktoria and University of Borås, Gothenburg, Sweden	Information Technology/Sustainable Transportation	2
Lin, C.K.	Institute of Computer and Communication Engineering, Department of Electrical Engineering, National Cheng Kung University Tainan, Taiwan	Electrical Engineering/Computer Science	2
Wang, T.H.	Center for Technologies of Ubiquitous Computing and Humanity, National Cheng Kung University, Tainan, Taiwan	Computer Science	2
Yang, J.F.	Institute of Computer and Communication Engineering, Department of Electrical Engineering, National Cheng Kung University, Tainan, Taiwan	Electrical Engineering/Computer Science	2
Luojus, S.	Laurea University of Applied Sciences, Vantaa, Finland	Service Innovation and Design/Computer Science	2
Lahti, J.	Laurea University of Applied Sciences, Vantaa, Finland	Service Innovation and Design/Computer Science	2

Authors that focus on this topic belong to three knowledge areas: Computer Science, Information Technology and Economics (Table 5). Some authors such as Yoshida, Lee and Choi belong to two knowledge areas, Economics (focus in the open innovation research) and Information Technology or Computer Science (focus in the open data research). The affiliations of the top authors are Japanese (six), Swedish (four), Spanish (three), Finnish (three), Korean (three) and Taiwanese (three).

3.2. Studied Themes by Knowledge Area

We analysed the knowledge areas considering the SJR subject areas and categories. In the Information Technology and Computer Science knowledge areas, topics such as the development of open innovation processes through web platforms are the most commonly studied [72,73]; other topics include the impact of the use of open government data to improve or produce new products and services, as well as the open innovation processes derived from the use of these data [71]. This last topic has also been addressed in knowledge areas such as Public Administration, along with other topics such as open data, transparency, civic engagement, and public sector innovation [10].

Regarding the knowledge areas of Systems Engineering, Electronic Engineering, Electrical Engineering, the most prevalent topics are the development of systems that offer a service to the user and that enlist the collaboration of these users to improve the product, thus involving various stakeholders in a co-creation process [56]. For Technology Management and Innovation, topics addressed include the management of technology innovation processes in organisations [32], or the phenomena of co-creation and innovation promotion [75].

In the knowledge areas of Medicine, Molecular Medicine, Pharmacology and Chemoinformatics, the positive impact of open data and open innovation on drug discovery and development processes is analysed [77,79]. Lastly, in Museology, the impetus of open data and open innovation in museums, libraries and archives is discussed [63].

3.3. Methodological Characteristics of the Documents

To perform a more in-depth literature review, this section presents an analysis of the methodological characteristics of the documents studied as the type of study, the analytical techniques, the source of information and the geographical area.

Analysing the type of documents indicates that 65.5% (36) are empirical and approximately 34.5% (19) are theoretical. Several aspects of the empirical documents have been analysed, such as the type of study (Table 6), analytical techniques used (Table 7), and sources of information (Table 8).

Tables 6 and 7 show that 61% (22) of the empirical documents are exclusively qualitative studies using the analytical technique of case study. On the other hand, six documents (approximately 17%) are exclusively quantitative, using analytical techniques such as the varimax rotation method, correlation coefficients, Cronbach's alpha coefficient, regression analysis, structural equation modelling, and descriptive statistics. Furthermore, seven documents (approximately 19.4%) use a combination of quantitative and qualitative techniques. All are case studies with various types of descriptive statistics, except for one by Smith & Sandberg, 2018 [69], that combines a case study with a cross-tabulation matrix. If we analyse all the studies that are exclusively quantitative or that are combined with a qualitative study, 13 documents are found (36% of the empirical documents). Eight of these are cross-sectional studies for the same period, and five are longitudinal studies.

Table 6. Type of study/author/s, year.

Type of Study	Author/s, Year
Quantitative	Herala, Vanhala, Porras & Kärri, 2016 [12]; Lee, Ham & Choi, 2016 [54]; Tossavainen, Shiramatsu, Ozono & Shintani, 2016 [73]; Fortunato, Gorgoglione, Messeni Petruzzelli & Panniello, 2017 [39]; Kuhlman, Ramamurthy, Sattigeri, Lozano, Cao, Reddy, Mojsilovic & Varshney, 2017 [53]; Väyrynen, Helander & Vasell, 2017 [75]
Qualitative	Conradie, Mulder & Choenni, 2012 [28]; Zdrazil, Blomberg & Ecker, 2012 [79]; Chan, 2013 [33]; De Freitas & Dacorso, 2014 [36]; Hoel, 2014 [45]; Cândido, Vianna, Gauthier, Aradas & Koslovsky, 2015 [32]; Hellberg & Hedström, 2015 [43]; Jaakola, Kekkonen, Lahti & Manninen, 2015 [48]; Katsonis & Botros, 2015 [50]; Lin, 2015 [55]; Perkmann & Schildt, 2015 [64]; Shiramatsu, Tossavainen, Ozono & Shintani, 2015 [68]; Zimmermann & Pucihar, 2015 [27]; Kauppinen, Luojus & Lahti, 2016 [52]; Nikiforov & Singireja, 2016 [60]; Owens, 2016 [63]; Gagliardi, Schina, Sarcinella, Mangialardi, Niglia & Corallo, 2017 [40]; Kassen, 2017 [10]; Luojus, Kauppinen, Lahti & Tahtinen, 2017 [59]; Huber, Wainwright & Rentocchini, 2018 [46]; Saxena, 2018 [67]; Tucci, Viscusi & Gautschi, 2018 [74]
Quantitative and qualitative	Hjalmarsson, Johannesson, Juell-Skielse & Rudmark, 2014 [44]; Juell-Skielse, Hjalmarsson, Juell-Skielse, Johannesson & Rudmark, 2014 [49]; Susha, Grönlund & Janssen, 2015 [71]; López de Ipiña, Emaldi, Aguilera & Pérez Velasco, 2016 [58]; Chatfield & Reddick, 2017 [34]; Emaldi, Aguilera, López-de-Ipiña & Pérez-Velasco, 2017 [38]; Smith & Sandberg, 2018 [69]

Table 7. Analytical techniques/author/s, year.

Analytical Techniques	Author/s, Year
Varimax rotation method	Väyrynen, Helander & Vasell, 2017 [75]
Correlation coefficients	Tossavainen, Shiramatsu, Ozono & Shintani, 2016 [73]; Kuhlman, Ramamurthy, Sattigeri, Lozano, Cao, Reddy, Mojsilovic & Varshney, 2017 [53]; Väyrynen, Helander & Vasell, 2017 [75]
Case study	Conradie, Mulder & Choenni, 2012 [28]; Zdrazil, Blomberg & Ecker, 2012 [79]; Chan, 2013 [33]; De Freitas & Dacorso, 2014 [36]; Hjalmarsson, Johannesson, Juell-Skielse & Rudmark, 2014 [44]; Juell-Skielse, Hjalmarsson, Juell-Skielse, Johannesson & Rudmark, 2014 [49]; Hoel, 2014 [45]; Hellberg & Hedström, 2015 [43]; Jaakola, Kekkonen, Lahti & Manninen, 2015 [48]; Katsonis & Botros, 2015 [50]; Lin, 2015 [55]; Perkmann & Schildt, 2015 [64]; Shiramatsu, Tossavainen, Ozono & Shintani, 2015 [68]; Susha, Grönlund & Janssen, 2015 [71]; Zimmermann & Pucihar, 2015 [27]; Kauppinen, Luojus & Lahti, 2016 [52]; López de Ipiña, Emaldi, Aguilera & Pérez Velasco, 2016 [58]; Nikiforov & Singireja, 2016 [60]; Owens, 2016 [63]; Chatfield & Reddick, 2017 [34]; Emaldi, Aguilera, López-de-Ipiña & Pérez-Velasco, 2017 [38]; Gagliardi, Schina, Sarcinella, Mangialardi, Niglia & Corallo, 2017 [40]; Kassen, 2017 [10]; Luojus, Kauppinen, Lahti & Tahtinen, 2017 [59]; Huber, Wainwright & Rentocchini, 2018 [46]; Saxena, 2018 [67]; Smith & Sandberg, 2018 [69]; Tucci, Viscusi & Gautschi, 2018 [74]
Cross tabulation matrix	Smith & Sandberg, 2018 [69]
Cronbach's alpha coefficient	Väyrynen, Helander & Vasell, 2017 [75]
Descriptive statistics	Hjalmarsson, Johannesson, Juell-Skielse & Rudmark, 2014 [44]; Juell-Skielse, Hjalmarsson, Juell-Skielse, Johannesson & Rudmark, 2014 [49]; Susha, Grönlund & Janssen, 2015 [71]; Herala, Vanhala, Porras & Kärri, 2016 [12]; Lee, Ham & Choi, 2016 [54]; López de Ipiña, Emaldi, Aguilera & Pérez Velasco, 2016 [58]; Chatfield & Reddick, 2017 [34]; Emaldi, Aguilera, López-de-Ipiña & Pérez-Velasco, 2017 [38]; Väyrynen, Helander & Vasell, 2017 [75]
Other qualitative studies	Cândido, Vianna, Gauthier, Aradas & Koslovsky, 2015 [32]
Regression analyses	Fortunato, Gorgoglione, Messeni Petruzzelli & Panniello, 2017 [39]; Kuhlman, Ramamurthy, Sattigeri, Lozano, Cao, Reddy, Mojsilovic & Varshney, 2017 [53]; Väyrynen, Helander & Vasell, 2017 [75]
Structural equation modeling	Lee, Ham & Choi, 2016 [54]

The most prevalent analytical technique used is the case study, identified in 28 documents (77.8% of the empirical studies), followed by descriptive statistics found in nine documents (25% of the empirical studies) (Table 6).

Table 8 presents the information sources used in the empirical studies. Most (28, or 77.8%) of the documents analysed have a secondary source; 16 documents (44.4%) have only one source; and 8 documents (22.2%) have three or more sources. Primary sources are found in 18 (50%) of the empirical studies; 8 (22.2%) have a single primary source and 9 (25%) have two primary sources.

Table 9 shows that 60% of the documents (33) correspond to a single geographic area, while 18.2% (10) correspond to several geographic areas. Approximately 21.8% (12) of the documents do not indicate any geographic scope. The geographic areas represented are widely scattered, although approximately 53% (29) of those that indicate a geographic area are analyses conducted in Europe.

Table 8. Sources of information/author/s, year.

Sources of Information	Author/s, Year
1 primary	Lin, 2015 [55]; Shiramatsu, Tossavainen, Ozono & Shintani, 2015 [68]; Susha, Grönlund & Janssen, 2015 [71]; Tossavainen, Shiramatsu, Ozono & Shintani, 2016 [73]; Chatfield & Reddick, 2017 [34]; Huber, Wainwright & Rentocchini, 2018 [46]; Smith & Sandberg, 2018 [69]; Tucci, Viscusi & Gautschi, 2018 [74]
2 primary	Conradie, Mulder & Choenni, 2012 [28]; Hjalmarsson, Johannesson, Juell-Skielse & Rudmark, 2014 [44]; Juell-Skielse, Hjalmarsson, Juell-Skielse, Johannesson & Rudmark, 2014 [49]; Perkmann & Schildt, 2015 [64]; Kauppinen, Luojus & Lahti, 2016 [52]; López de Ipiña, Emaldi, Aguilera & Pérez Velasco, 2016 [58]; Emaldi, Aguilera, López-de-Ipiña & Pérez-Velasco, 2017 [38]; Luojus, Kauppinen, Lahti & Tahtinen, 2017 [59]; Väyrynen, Helander & Vasell, 2017 [75]
3 or more primary	Hellberg & Hedström, 2015 [43]
1 secondary	Zdrazil, Blomberg & Ecker, 2012 [79]; Chan, 2013 [33]; De Freitas & Dacorso, 2014 [36]; Hjalmarsson, Johannesson, Juell-Skielse & Rudmark, 2014 [44]; Hoel, 2014 [45]; Juell-Skielse, Johannesson, Juell-Skielse, Johannesson & Rudmark, 2014 [49]; Hellberg & Hedström, 2015 [43]; Jaakola, Kekkonen, Lahti & Manninen, 2015 [48]; Lin, 2015 [55]; Kauppinen, Luojus & Lahti, 2016 [52]; Nikiforov & Singireja, 2016 [60]; Owens, 2016 [63]; Gagliardi, Schina, Sarcinella, Mangialardi, Niglia & Corallo, 2017 [40]; Luojus, Kauppinen, Lahti & Tahtinen, 2017 [59]; Smith & Sandberg, 2018 [69]; Tucci, Viscusi & Gautschi, 2018 [74]
2 secondary	Herala, Vanhala, Porras & Kärri, 2016 [12]; Chatfield & Reddick, 2017 [34]; Kuhlman, Ramamurthy, Sattigeri, Lozano, Cao, Reddy, Mojsilovic & Varshney, 2017 [53]; Huber, Wainwright & Rentocchini, 2018 [46]
3 or more secondary	Katsonis & Botros, 2015 [50]; Perkmann & Schildt, 2015 [64]; Zimmermann & Pucihar, 2015 [27]; Lee, Ham & Choi, 2016 [54]; Noda, Honda, Yoshida & Coughlan, 2016 [62]; Fortunato, Gorgoglione, Messeni Petruzzelli & Panniello, 2017 [39]; Kassen, 2017 [10]; Saxena, 2018 [67]

Table 9. Geographical area/author/s, year.

Geographical Area	Author/s, Year
One geographical area	
Australia	Chatfield & Reddick, 2017 [34]
Brazil	De Freitas & Dacorso, 2014 [36]
Canada	Gold, 2016 [41]
Ecuador	Piedra, Chicaiza, Lopez-Vargas & Caro, 2016 [65]
European Union	Zdrazil, Blomberg & Ecker, 2012 [79]; Hoel, 2014 [45]
Finland	Jaakkola, Mäkinen, Henno & Mäkelä, 2014 [48]; Jaakola, Kekkonen, Lahti & Manninen, 2015 [47]; Kauppinen, Luojus & Lahti, 2016 [52]; Luojus, Kauppinen, Lahti & Tahtinen, 2017 [59]; Väyrynen, Helander & Vasell, 2017 [75]
India	Saxena, 2018 [67]
Ireland	Stephenson, Di Lorenzo & Aonghusa, 2012 [70]

Table 9. *Cont.*

Geographical Area	Author/s, Year
Italy	Fortunato, Gorgoglione, Messeni Petruzzelli & Panniello, 2017 [39]; Gagliardi, Schina, Sarcinella, Mangialardi, Niglia & Corallo, 2017 [40]
Japan	Tossavainen, Shiramatsu, Ozono & Shintani, 2014 [72]; Shiramatsu, Tossavainen, Ozono & Shintani, 2015 [68]; Tossavainen, Shiramatsu, Ozono & Shintani, 2016 [73]
Kazakhstan	Kassen, 2017 [10]
Netherlands	Conradie, Mulder & Choenni, 2012 [28]
Singapore	Chan, 2013 [33]
Sweden	Hjalmarsson, Johannesson, Juell-Skielse & Rudmark, 2014 [44]; Hellberg & Hedström, 2015 [43]; Smith & Sandberg, 2018 [69]
Switzerland	Dardier, 2018 [35]; Tucci, Viscusi & Gautschi, 2018 [74]
Spain	López de Ipiña, Emaldi, Aguilera & Pérez Velasco, 2016 [58]; Emaldi, Aguilera, López-de-Ipiña & Pérez-Velasco, 2017 [38]
Taiwan	Lin, Wang & Yang, 2012 [56]; Lin, Wang & Yang, 2013 [57]
United Kingdom	Lin, 2015 [55]; Huber, Wainwright & Rentocchini, 2018 [46]
United States	Owens, 2016 [63]
Many geographical areas	
Australia and United Kingdom	Katsonis & Botros, 2015 [50]
Australia, New Zealand, European Union and Japan	Noda, Honda, Yoshida & Coughlan, 2016 [62]
France, Italy, Belgium, Germany, Poland and Greece	Del Frate, Mothe, Barbier, Becker, Olszewski & Soudris, 2017 [37]
Sweden and Netherlands	Susha, Grönlund & Janssen, 2015 [71]
United Kingdom, Canada and Sweden	Perkmann & Schildt, 2015 [64]
United States and Russia	Nikiforov & Singireja, 2016 [60]
United States and Switzerland	Zimmermann & Pucihar, 2015 [27]
>10 Geographical areas	Juell-Skielse, Hjalmarsson, Juell-Skielse, Johannesson & Rudmark, 2014 [49]; Lee, Ham & Choi, 2016 [54]; Kuhlman, Ramamurthy, Sattigeri, Lozano, Cao, Reddy, Mojsilovic & Varshney, 2017 [53]

4. Discussion

After analysing the characteristics of previous literature that jointly analyses open data and open innovation, we discuss the different knowledge areas focused on this topic. We observe that open data and open innovation studies are addressing the topic from different perspectives. While open data has been analysed under the Computer Science, Engineering and Public Administration disciplines, open innovation has been developed in the Management and Innovation subjects. Subsequently, we develop these arguments according to the knowledge areas identified in our analysis.

Knowledge areas such as Information Technology and Computer Science help to understand how the data must be (characteristics, quality . . . .) and the format in which data have to be published for performing open innovation. Additionally, we think that it is necessary to deepen the study of the data publishing mediums (platforms, webs . . .) and their utility for performing open innovation. On the other hand, it is interesting to know how the data can be reused for performing open innovation. So, literature focused on the Public Administration area offers a framework which allows us to analyse the ecosystem of reusers and the products and services that can be obtained under the open innovation paradigm.

Regarding the Management and Innovation subjects, previous literature shows theoretical open innovation models that can be adapted for studying the use of open data for performing open innovation. More empirical studies that develop applications about this topic are necessary. In some knowledge areas such as Systems Engineering, Electronic Engineering, Electrical Engineering, Medicine, Molecular Medicine, Pharmacology and Chemoinformatics, and Museology, the case study methodology is too frequent. These papers offer cases or examples of open innovation activities obtained from open data.

In our descriptive analysis, we have found no documents about the state of the art about open data and open innovation jointly. Even though the previous literature focuses on the study of some specific aspects in different knowledge areas, there are no papers that develop theoretical frameworks that help to understand the use of open data for generating open innovation.

In this context, we have developed a theoretical model, which includes some dimensions of previous models of open data and open innovation. On the one hand, following Abella et al. (2019) [80], we have used the open data impact process and the reusers categories of open data. The model presents a process with four phases: 1. Candidate data; 2. Published data; 3. Reused data; and 4. Impact; and proposes a classification of data reusers in three groups: (1) primary open data source (public organizations and other related organizations that publish open data); (2) direct reusers (social and professional); and (3) end users (social, citizen, professional and academic). On the other hand, following Gassmann and Enkel (2004) [81] and Nerone, Canciglieri Junior, Steiner and Young (2014) [82], we have considered two types of open innovation: inbound (to insource external ideas and technologies to enhance products' values) and outbound (to outsource internal resources for refining, exploiting and bringing them to market). We also consider the two types together, or coupled (a combination of the inbound and outbound processes). Our model is the first theoretical proposal for the study of the use of open data for open innovation (Table 10).

Table 10. Theoretical model: Open data impact process for open innovation.

Theoretical Model		Open Data Impact Process			
		Phase 1: Candidate Data	Phase 2: Published Data	Phase 3: Reused Data	Phase 4: Impact
Open innovation and the reusers categories	Type What kind of open innovation can be developed with open data?	Outbound To select internal data from different agents (public organizations, smart cities …) to be opened	Outbound To offer the open data from different agents (public organizations, smart cities …)	Inbound To reuse external open data to innovate, creating products and services Coupled To combine internal data and open data to innovate	Outbound Inbound Coupled To analyse the social, economic and technologic impact of using open data for developing the three types of open innovation
	Agent type Who performs open innovation?	Primary open data source Public organizations and other related organizations	Primary open data source Public organizations and other related organizations	Direct reusers Social and professional End users Social, citizen, professional and academic	Primary open data source Direct reusers End users

5. Conclusions

There is growing interest from both academic and professional scenarios of studying the innovation topic under the perspective of openness [83] and the reuse of open data [80]. One of the main effects of this reuse is the possibility of innovating and creating new businesses or developing new products or services for citizens [8,9]. Therefore, these two concepts are fully related and it is necessary to deepen, from the academic context, in their joint study in order to guide to the managers to take advantage of open data and open innovation.

Literature reviews are very useful to know the state of the art about a topic. In this sense, we have found some literature reviews about open data or open innovation, but there are still no studies that jointly analyse both topics. This paper tries to cover this gap in the literature by formulating three research questions. To this aim, we have carried out a search of the papers that include open data and open innovation research. We have identified just 55 documents. Many of them are in the initial stages of the research because they are conference papers. It seems logical to say that the joint study of these two topics is emerging and that several documents have not yet been published but are being presented in various academic and professional forums.

To answer the first research question, two analyses have been carried out. Firstly, we have identified the main journals and conferences that publish papers on these topics. The results show that the documents are published in journals of different knowledge areas, Computer Science and Engineering and Public Administration that analyse the issue of open data. Other knowledge areas are focused on open innovation such as Business, Management and Accounting or on the practical applications that have the use of open data to perform open innovation, as is the case of applications or examples of its use in knowledge areas related to Health Sciences, Engineering or the knowledge area of Museology. Secondly, the paper identifies the authors that have published in these issues. It is observed that there is still little productivity per author (maximum three articles), which confirms that this line of research is in its initial stages. The authors are related to knowledge areas as Computer Science, Information Technology and Economics. If we consider their affiliation, the authors of research institutions of Japanese, Korean or Taiwanese universities stand out. There is also a presence of European researchers (Spanish, Finnish and Swedish) among the top authors.

To answer the second research question, knowledge areas are analysed. The main conclusion is the multidisciplinary character of this topic. The most outstanding knowledge areas are Information Technology and Computer Science. Also, from other areas such as Public Administration, Business and Management, and Medicine, papers are being carried out focused on aspects more related to management issues and the application of open data to open innovation.

Regarding the third research question, it is observed that although it is an emerging topic, most of the papers (65.5%) are empirical. This result highlights the need to carry out more theoretical studies that help lay the foundations and the theoretical bases to jointly study these two issues. Moreover, most of the empirical papers are qualitative (61%), which is consistent with the state of development of the research line. The most used technique is the case study. This methodology helps to understand, solve or improve a professional world procedure [84] and is appropriate when the phenomenon investigated is exploratory and descriptive and when primary information is available. As the literature is not conclusive, it is necessary to carry out an in-depth and qualitative analysis on the topic. In this sense, it is observed that 50% of the articles analysed use primary information sources and there are some that combine primary and secondary. The case method also allows applying the inductive method to propose propositions or theoretical hypotheses based on practical experience and examples of application of open data use to open innovation. Finally, results show that the studies have been carried out in different geographical areas. This shows the global reach of these issues, which, besides being applicable in different areas of knowledge, are also applicable in different geographical areas.

The joint analysis of open data and open innovation can be studied considering three dimensions: (1) the main phases of the open data process, (2) the types of open innovation that can be developed with open data, and (3) the ecosystems of reusers that are the agents that make the open innovation possible. In that sense, we have proposed a theoretical model to analyse the open data impact process for open innovation. This model can be a guide to future research and help us to present some future research lines and questions. Future research can analyse the following questions for each phase of our theoretical model (Table 10). Phase 1: How does outbound open innovation select the candidate open data? What is the role of public administrations in the selection of open data for outbound open innovation? What effect do the open data policies of each country have on the opportunities to perform open innovation by both public and private institutions? How can the FAIR principles for scientific data—findable, accessible, interoperable and reusable—[85] be adapted to the context of open data for open innovation? Phase 2: How does outbound open innovation publish open data? What is the role of public administrations in the publication of open data for outbound open innovation? How can models developed for innovation in open science such as European Open Science Cloud (EOSC) [86] be adapted to the open data for the open innovation context? Phase 3: What forms of open data reuse are more suitable for open innovation? What is the inbound innovation of each reuser like? and Phase 4: What economic and social effect does the use of open data have in making open innovation? What is the social, economic and technological impact of each type of open innovation? What is the social, economic and technological impact for each reuser? And, in addition, some future research is necessary to develop theoretical and practical applications and examples from a holistic perspective considering all the aspects included in our theoretical model. In that sense, other research questions have been raised by our study. What topics have been the most studied? What are the theories that can be applied to study this phenomenon? What opportunities for open innovation do open data offer? What are the barriers when using open data for open innovation?

This paper presents some theoretical and practical implications. The paper analyses the main aspects of the previous literature that has combined the terms open data and open innovation: journals, conferences, authors, knowledge areas and methodological characteristics. Our results are useful for researchers who start to research this topic because they identify existing gaps and propose new research questions. In addition, "open innovation can help to identify opportunities for entrepreneurs" [87] (p. 2). In that sense, the paper can be useful as a starting point for agents such as citizens, companies or public institutions that want to carry out an open innovation activity such as the creation of digital applications and services through the reuse of open data.

Finally, the paper has some limitations. Other techniques can also be used in order to complete the descriptive analysis, such as bibliometric techniques (bibliographic coupling, co-citation analysis or co-author analysis) that would provide additional information and alternative approaches to describe how state-of-the-art this topic is.

Funding: This research was funded by the Spanish Ministry of Economy and Competitiveness [grant number ECO2015-67434-R].

Conflicts of Interest: The authors declare no conflict of interest.

References

1. Smith, M.L.; Seward, R. Openness as Social Praxis. *First Monday* **2017**, *22*. [CrossRef]
2. Chesbrough, H.W. *Open Innovation: The New Imperative for Creating and Profiting from Technology*; Harvard Business School Press: Boston, MA, USA, 2003.
3. Chesbrough, H.W. The Era of Open Innovation. *MIT Sloan Manag. Rev.* **2003**, *44*, 35–41.
4. Chesbrough, H.W. New Puzzles and New Findings. In *Open Innovation: Researching a New Paradigm*; Chesbrough, H.W., Vanhaverbeke, W., Wes, J., Eds.; Oxford University Press: Oxford, UK, 2006; pp. 15–33.
5. European Data Portal. Available online: https://www.europeandataportal.eu/elearning/en/module1/#/id/co-01 (accessed on 4 January 2019).
6. Wallace, N.; Castro, D. The State of Data Innovation in the EU. Center for Data Innovation 2017. Available online: http://www2.datainnovation.org/2017-data-innovation-eu.pdf (accessed on 4 January 2019).

7. Berends, J.; Carrara, W.; Engbers, W.; Vollers, H. Re-Using Open Data. A Study on Companies Transforming Open Data into Economic and Societal Value. European Commission. Directorate General for Communications Networks, Content and Technology 2017. Available online: https://www.europeandataportal.eu/sites/default/files/re-using_open_data.pdf (accessed on 4 January 2019).
8. Abella, A.; Ortiz-de-Urbina-Criado, M.; De-Pablos-Heredero, C. Information Reuse in Smart Cities' Ecosystems. *Prof. Inform.* **2015**, *24*, 838–844. [CrossRef]
9. Abella, A.; Ortiz-de-Urbina-Criado, M.; De-Pablos-Heredero, C. A Model for the Analysis of Data-Driven Innovation and Value Generation in Smart Cities' Ecosystems. *Cities* **2017**, *64*, 47–53. [CrossRef]
10. Kassen, M. Open Data in Kazakhstan: Incentives, Implementation and Challenges. *Inf. Technol. People* **2017**, *30*, 301–323. [CrossRef]
11. Jetzek, T.; Avital, M.; Bjorn-Andersen, N. Data-Driven Innovation through Open Government Data. *J. Theor. Appl. Electron. Commer. Res.* **2014**, *9*, 100–120. [CrossRef]
12. Herala, A.; Vanhala, E.; Porras, J.; Kärri, T. Experiences about Opening Data in Private Sector: A Systematic Literature Review. In Proceedings of the SAI Computing Conference, London, UK, 13–15 July 2016; pp. 715–724. [CrossRef]
13. Hossain, M.A.; Dwivedi, Y.K.; Rana, N.P. State-of-the-Art in Open Data Research: Insights from Existing Literature and a Research Agenda. *J. Organ. Comp. Electron. Commer.* **2016**, *26*, 14–40. [CrossRef]
14. Corrales-Garay, D.; Ortiz-de-Urbina-Criado, M.; Mora-Valentín, E.-M. Knowledge Areas, Themes and Future Research on Open Data: A Co-Word Analysis. *Gov. Inf. Q.* **2019**, *36*, 77–87. [CrossRef]
15. Zhang, Y.; Hua, W.; Yuan, S. Mapping the Scientific Research on Open Data: A Bibliometric Review. *Learn. Publ.* **2018**, *31*, 95–106. [CrossRef]
16. Su, H.N.; Lee, P.C. Framing the Structure of Global Open Innovation Research. *J. Inform.* **2012**, *6*, 202–216. [CrossRef]
17. Remneland Wikhamn, B.; Wikhamn, W. Structuring of the Open Innovation Field. *J. Technol. Manag. Innov.* **2013**, *8*, 173–185. [CrossRef]
18. Kovács, A.; Van Looy, B.; Cassiman, B. Exploring the Scope of Open Innovation: A Bibliometric Review of a Decade of Research. *Scientometrics* **2015**, *104*, 951–983. [CrossRef]
19. Hossain, M.; Anees-ur-Rehman, M. Open Innovation: An Analysis of Twelve Years of Research. *Strateg. Outsourc.* **2016**, *9*, 22–37. [CrossRef]
20. Hossain, M.; Islam, K.M.Z.; Sayeed, M.A.; Kauranen, I. A Comprehensive Review of Open Innovation Literature. *J. Sci Technol. Policy Manag.* **2016**, *7*, 2–25. [CrossRef]
21. Hossain, M.; Kauranen, I. Open Innovation in SMEs: A Systematic Literature Review. *J. Strat. Manag.* **2016**, *9*, 58–73. [CrossRef]
22. Randhawa, K.; Wilden, R.; Hohberger, J. A Bibliometric Review of Open Innovation: Setting a Research Agenda. *J. Prod. Innov. Manag.* **2016**, *33*, 750–772. [CrossRef]
23. De Paulo, A.F.; Carvalho, L.C.; Costa, M.T.G.V.; Lopes, J.E.F.; Galina, S.V.R. Mapping Open Innovation: A Bibliometric Review to Compare Developed and Emerging Countries. *Glob. Bus. Rev.* **2017**, *18*, 291–307. [CrossRef]
24. Ale Ebrahim, N.; Bong, Y. Open Innovation: A Bibliometric Study. *Int J. Innov.* **2017**, *5*, 411–420. [CrossRef]
25. Lopes, A.P.V.B.V.; De Carvalho, M.M. Evolution of the Open Innovation Paradigm: Towards a Contingent Conceptual Model. *Technol. Forecast. Soc. Chang.* **2018**, *132*, 284–298. [CrossRef]
26. Krishnamurthy, R.; Awazu, Y. Liberating Data for Public Value: The Case of Data.gov. *Int. J. Inf. Manag.* **2016**, *36*, 668–672. [CrossRef]
27. Zimmermann, H.; Pucihar, A. Open Innovation, Open Data and New Business Models. In *Schriftenreihe Informatik, Information Technology and Society Interaction and Interdependence*, Proceedings of the 23rd Annual Interdisciplinary Information Management Talks Conference (IDIMT), Podebrady, Czech Republic, 9–11 September 2015; Petr, D., Gerhard, C., Vaclav, O., Eds.; Universitatsverlag Rudolf Trauner: Linz, Austria, 2015; Volume 44, pp. 449–458. [CrossRef]
28. Conradie, P.; Mulder, I.; Choenni, S. Rotterdam Open Data: Exploring the Release of Public Sector Information through Co-Creation. In Proceedings of the 18th International Conference on Engineering, Technology and Innovation (ICE), Munich, Germany, 18–20 June 2012. [CrossRef]

29. Marin-Garcia, J.A.; Alfalla-Luque, R. Protocol: Is there Agreement or Disagreement between the Absolute and Relative Impact Indices Obtained from the Web of Science and Scopus Data? *Working Pap. Oper. Manag.* **2018**, *9*, 53–80. [CrossRef]
30. Bonazzi, R.; Liu, Z. Two Birds with One Stone. An Economically Viable Solution for Linked Open Data Platforms. In Proceedings of the 28th Bled eConference: #eWellbeing, Bled, Slovenia, 7–10 June 2015; pp. 77–85. [CrossRef]
31. Boubin, J. Importance of Open Innovation Mode for Start-Up Projects. In Proceedings of the International Scientific Conference of Business Economics, Management and Marketing (ISCOBEMM), Zajeci, Czech Republic, 25–26 May 2017; Janosova, L., Kuchynkova, L., Cenek, M., Eds.; Masarykova University: Brno, Czech Republic, 2017; pp. 36–43.
32. Cândido, A.P.; Vianna, C.T.; Gauthier, F.O.; Aradas, A.R.P.; Koslovsky, M.A.N. Proposta de Modelo para Avaliação e Supervisão de Gestão da Inovação Tecnológica em Pequenas e Médias Organizações. *Espacios* **2015**, *36*, 8.
33. Chan, C.M.L. From Open Data to Open Innovation Strategies: Creating e-Services using Open Government Data. In Proceedings of the 46th Annual Hawaii International Conference on System Sciences, Maui, HI, USA, 7–10 January 2013; Sprague, R.H., Ed.; IEEE: New York, NY, USA, 2013; pp. 1890–1899. [CrossRef]
34. Chatfield, A.T.; Reddick, C.G. A Longitudinal Cross-Sector Analysis of Open Data Portal Service Capability: The Case of Australian Local Governments. *Gov. Inf. Q.* **2017**, *34*, 231–243. [CrossRef]
35. Dardier, G.J. Open Access to Digital Information at the University for Applied Sciences and Arts Western Switzerland. In *ACM International Conference Proceeding Series, Proceedings of the 1st International Conference on Digital Tools and Uses Congress (DTUC), Paris, France, 3–5 October 2018*; Siala-Kallel, F., Reyes, E., Kembellec, G., Szoniecky, S., Labelle, S., Mkadmi, A., Fournier-S'niehotta, R., Ammi, M., Eds.; ACM: New York, NY, USA, 2018. [CrossRef]
36. De Freitas, R.K.V.; Dacorso, A.L.R. Open Innovation in Public Management: Analysis of the Brazilian Action Plan for Open Government Partnership. *Rev. Adm. Pública* **2014**, *48*, 869–888. [CrossRef]
37. Del Frate, F.; Mothe, J.; Barbier, C.; Becker, M.; Olszewski, R.; Soudris, D. FabSpace 2.0: The Open-Innovation Network for Geodata-Driven Innovation. In Proceedings of the 37th Annual IEEE International Geoscience and Remote Sensing Symposium (IGARSS), Forth Worth, TX, USA, 23–27 July 2017; IEEE: New York, NY, USA, 2017; pp. 353–356. [CrossRef]
38. Emaldi, M.; Aguilera, U.; López-de-Ipiña, D.; Pérez-Velasco, J. Towards Citizen Co-Created Public Service Apps. *Sensors* **2017**, *17*, 1265. [CrossRef] [PubMed]
39. Fortunato, A.; Gorgoglione, M.; Messeni Petruzzelli, A.; Panniello, U. Leveraging Big Data for Sustaining Open Innovation: The Case of Social TV. *Inf. Syst. Manag.* **2017**, *34*, 238–249. [CrossRef]
40. Gagliardi, D.; Schina, L.; Sarcinella, M.L.; Mangialardi, G.; Niglia, F.; Corallo, A. Information and Communication Technologies and Public Participation: Interactive Maps and Value Added for Citizens. *Gov. Inf. Q.* **2017**, *34*, 153–166. [CrossRef]
41. Gold, E.R. Accelerating Translational Research through Open Science: The Neuro Experiment. *PLoS Biol.* **2016**, *14*, e2001259. [CrossRef]
42. Ham, J.; Lee, J.N.; Kim, D.J.; Choi, B. Open Innovation Maturity Model for the Government: An Open System Perspective. In Proceedings of the International Conference on Information Systems: Exploring the Information Frontier (ICIS), Forth Worth, TX, USA, 13–16 December 2015.
43. Hellberg, A.S.; Hedström, K. The Story of the Sixth Myth of Open Data and Open Government. *Transform. Gov. People Process Policy* **2015**, *9*, 35–51. [CrossRef]
44. Hjalmarsson, A.; Johannesson, P.; Juell-Skielse, G.; Rudmark, D. Beyond Innovation Contests: A Framework of Barriers to Open Innovation of Digital Services. In Proceedings of the 22nd European Conference on Information Systems (ECIS), Tel Aviv, Israel, 9–11 June 2014.
45. Hoel, T. Standards as Enablers for Innovation in Education—The Breakdown of European Pre-Standardisation. In Proceedings of the 6th ITU Kaleidoscope Academic Conference: Living in a Converged World—Impossible Without Standards? St. Petersburg, Russia, 3–5 June 2014; IEEE: New York, NY, USA, 2014. [CrossRef]
46. Huber, F.; Wainwright, T.; Rentocchini, F. Open Data for Open Innovation: Managing Absorptive Capacity in SMEs. *R D Manag.* **2018**. [CrossRef]

47. Jaakola, A.; Kekkonen, H.; Lahti, T.; Manninen, A. Open Data, Open Cities: Experiences from the Helsinki Metropolitan Area. Case Helsinki Region Infoshare www.hri.fi. *Stat. J. IAOS* **2015**, *31*, 117–122. [CrossRef]
48. Jaakkola, H.; Mäkinen, T.; Henno, J.; Mäkelä, J. Open^n. In Proceedings of the 37th International Convention on Information and Communication Technology, Electronics and Microelectronics (MIPRO), Opatija, Croatia, 26–30 May 2014; Biljanovic, P., Butkovic, Z., Skala, K., Golubic, S., Cicin Sain, M., Sruk, V., Ribaric, S., Gros, S., Vrdoljak, B., Mauher, M., Cetusic, G., Eds.; IEEE: New York, NY, USA, 2014; pp. 608–615. [CrossRef]
49. Juell-Skielse, G.; Hjalmarsson, A.; Juell-Skielse, E.; Johannesson, P.; Rudmark, D. Contests as Innovation Intermediaries in Open Data Markets. *Inf. Polity* **2014**, *19*, 247–262. [CrossRef]
50. Katsonis, M.; Botros, A. Digital Government: A Primer and Professional Perspectives. *Aust. J. Public Adm.* **2015**, *74*, 42–52. [CrossRef]
51. Kauppinen, S. Enhancing Public e-Service Development with Citizens' Self-Organized Collaboration. In *Advances in Social and Behavioral Sciences, Proceedings of the SSR International Conference on Social Sciences and Information (SSR-SSI), Tokyo, Japan, 29–30 November 2015*; Abed Alasadi, H.A., Yabhoubi, H., Eds.; Singapore Management and Sport Science Institute: Singapore, 2015; Volume 10, pp. 212–217.
52. Kauppinen, S.; Luojus, S.; Lahti, J. Involving Citizens in Open Innovation Process by Means of Gamification: The Case of WeLive. In *ACM International Conference Proceeding Series, Proceedings of the 9th Nordic Conference on Human-Computer Interaction (NordiCHI), Gothenburg, Sweden, 23–27 October 2016*; ACM: New York, NY, USA, 2016. [CrossRef]
53. Kuhlman, C.; Ramamurthy, K.N.; Sattigeri, P.; Lozano, A.C.; Cao, L.; Reddy, C.; Mojsilovic, A.; Varshney, K.R. How to Foster Innovation: A Data-Driven Approach to Measuring Economic Competitiveness. *IBM J. Res. Dev.* **2017**, *61*. [CrossRef]
54. Lee, J.N.; Ham, J.; Choi, B. Effect of Government Data Openness on a Knowledge-Based Economy. *Procedia Comput. Sci.* **2016**, *91*, 158–167. [CrossRef]
55. Lin, Y. Open Data and Co-Production of Public Value of BBC Backstage. *Int. J. Digit. Telev.* **2015**, *6*, 145–162. [CrossRef]
56. Lin, C.K.; Wang, T.H.; Yang, J.F. TOUCH Doctor—A Nutrition Control Service System Developed under Living Lab Methodology. *Int. J. Autom. Smart Technol.* **2012**, *2*, 253–263. [CrossRef]
57. Lin, C.K.; Wang, T.H.; Yang, J.F. Developed Smart Nutrient Services with Living Lab Methodology. In Proceedings of the 1st International Conference on Orange Technologies (ICOT), Tainan, Taiwan, 12–16 March 2013; IEEE: New York, NY, USA, 2013; pp. 260–263. [CrossRef]
58. López-De-Ipiña, D.; Emaldi, P.; Aguilera, U.; Pérez-Velasco, J. Towards Citizen Co-Created Public Service Apps. In *Lecture Notes in Computer Science, Proceedings of the 10th International Conference on Ubiquitous Computing and Ambient Intelligence (UCAmI), San Bartolomé de Tirajana, Spain, 29 November–2 December 2016*; García, C.R., Caballero Gil, M., Burmester, M., Quesada Arencibia, A., Eds.; Springer: Cham, Switzerland; Volume 10070, pp. 469–481. [CrossRef]
59. Luojus, S.; Kauppinen, S.; Lahti, J.; Tahtinen, L. Forming Multidisciplinary Master's Degree Student Teams by Means of Gamification Case: The WeLive Design Game. In Proceedings of the 10th International Conference of Education, Research and Innovation (ICERI), Seville, Spain, 16–18 November 2017; Chova, L.G., Martínez, A.L., Torres, I.C., Eds.; International Academy of Technology, Education and Development (IATED): Valencia, Spain, 2017; pp. 1665–1673. [CrossRef]
60. Nikiforov, A.; Singireja, A. Open Data and Crowdsourcing Perspectives for Smart City in the United States and Russia. In ACM International Conference Proceeding Series, Proceedings of the 3rd International Conference on Electronic Governance and Open Society: Challenges in Eurasia (EGOSE), St Petersburg, Russia, 22–23 November 2016; ACM: New York, NY, USA, 2016; pp. 171–177. [CrossRef]
61. Noda, T.; Duan, R.; Fukushiro, H.; Yoshida, A.; Coughlan, S. The Classification, Challenge and Potential of Business Models by Using Open Data. In Proceedings of the 13th International Symposium on Open Collaboration (OpenSym), Galway, Ireland, 23–25 August 2017; ACM: New York, NY, USA, 2017. [CrossRef]
62. Noda, T.; Honda, M.; Yoshida, A.; Coughlan, S. Review of Estimation Method of Economic Effects Created by Using Open Data. In Proceedings of the 12th International Symposium on Open Collaboration (OpenSym), Berlin, Germany, 17–19 August 2016; ACM: New York, NY, USA, 2016. [CrossRef]
63. Owens, T. Curating in the Open: A Case for Iteratively and Openly Publishing Curatorial Research on the Web. *Curator* **2016**, *59*, 427–442. [CrossRef]

64. Perkmann, M.; Schildt, H. Open Data Partnerships between Firms and Universities: The Role of Boundary Organizations. *Res. Policy* **2015**, *44*, 1133–1143. [CrossRef]
65. Piedra, N.; Chicaiza, J.; Lopez-Vargas, J.; Caro, E.T. Guidelines to Producing Structured Interoperable Data from Open Access Repositories. In Proceedings of the 46th Annual Frontiers in Education Conference (FIE), Erie, PA, USA, 12–15 October 2016; IEEE: New York, NY, USA, 2016. [CrossRef]
66. Reisdorf, W.C.; Chhugani, N.; Sanseau, P.; Agarwal, P. Harnessing Public Domain Data to Discover and Validate Therapeutic Targets. *Expert. Opin. Drug Discov.* **2017**, *12*, 687–693. [CrossRef]
67. Saxena, S. Asymmetric Open Government Data (OGD) Framework in India. *Dig. Policy Regul. Gov.* **2018**, *20*, 434–448. [CrossRef]
68. Shiramatsu, S.; Tossavainen, T.; Ozono, T.; Shintani, T. Towards Continuous Collaboration on Civic Tech Projects: Use Cases of a Goal Sharing System Based on Linked Open Data. In *Lecture Notes in Computer Science, Electronic Participation, Proceedings of the 7th Annual International IFIP WG 8.5 Conference on Electronic Participation (ePart), Thessaloniki, Greece, 30 August–2 September 2015*; Tambouris, E., Panagiotopoulos, P., Saebo, O., Tarabanis, K., Wimmer, M.A., Milano, M., Pardo, T., Eds.; Springer: Berlin, Germany, 2015; Volume 9249, pp. 81–92. [CrossRef]
69. Smith, G.; Sandberg, J. Barriers to Innovating with Open Government Data: Exploring Experiences across Service Phases and User Types. *Inf. Polity* **2018**, *23*, 249–265. [CrossRef]
70. Stephenson, M.; Di Lorenzo, G.; Aonghusa, P.M. Open Innovation Portal: A Collaborative Platform for Open City Data Sharing. In Proceedings of the IEEE International Conference on Pervasive Computing and Communications Workshops (PERCOM Workshops), Lugano, Switzerland, 19–23 March 2012; pp. 522–524. [CrossRef]
71. Susha, I.; Grönlund, A.; Janssen, M. Driving Factors of Service Innovation using Open Government Data: An Exploratory Study of Entrepreneurs in Two Countries. *Inf. Polity* **2015**, *20*, 19–34. [CrossRef]
72. Tossavainen, T.; Shiramatsu, S.; Ozono, T.; Shintani, T. Implementing a System Enabling Open Innovation by Sharing Public Goals Based on Linked Open Data. In *Lecture Notes in Computer Science Modern Advances in Applied Intelligence, Proceedings of the 27th International Conference on Industrial, Engineering and Other Applications of Applied Intelligent Systems (IEA/AIE), Kaohsiung, Taiwan, 3–6 June 2014*; Ali, M., Pan, J.S., Chen, S.M., Horng, M.F., Eds.; Springer: Cham, Switzerland, 2014; Volume 8482, pp. 98–108. [CrossRef]
73. Tossavainen, T.; Shiramatsu, S.; Ozono, T.; Shintani, T. A Linked Open Data Based System Utilizing Structured Open Innovation Process for Addressing Collaboratively Public Concerns in Regional Societies. *Appl. Intell.* **2016**, *44*, 196–207. [CrossRef]
74. Tucci, C.; Viscusi, G.; Gautschi, H. Translating Science into Business Innovation: The Case of Open Food and Nutrition Data Hackathons. *Front. Nutr.* **2018**, *5*, 96. [CrossRef]
75. Väyrynen, H.; Helander, N.; Vasell, T. Knowledge Management for Open Innovation: Comparing Research Results between SMEs and Large Companies. *Int. J. Innov. Manag.* **2017**, *21*. [CrossRef]
76. Viseur, R. Open Science: Practical Issues in Open Research Data. In Proceedings of the 4th International Conference on Data Management Technologies and Applications (DATA), Colmar, Alsace, France, 20–22 July 2015; Belo, O., Helfert, M., Francalanci, C., Holzinger, A., Eds.; SciTePress: Setúbal, Portugal, 2015; pp. 201–2016. [CrossRef]
77. Wells, T.N.C.; Willis, P.; Burrows, J.N.; Van Huijsduijnen, R.H. Open Data in Drug Discovery and Development: Lessons from Malaria. *Nat. Rev. Drug Discov.* **2016**, *15*, 661–662. [CrossRef]
78. Yang, Z.; Kankanhalli, A. Innovation in Government Services: The Case of Open Data. In *Advances in Information and Communication Technology, Proceedings of the IFIP WG 8.6 International Working Conference on Transfer and Diffusion of IT (TDIT), Bangalore, India, 27–29 June 2013*; De, R., Wastell, D., Dwivedi, Y.K., Henriksen, H.Z., Eds.; Springer: New York, NY, USA, 2013; Volume 402, pp. 644–651. [CrossRef]
79. Zdrazil, B.; Blomberg, N.; Ecker, G.F. Taking Open Innovation to the Molecular Level—Strengths and Limitations. *Mol. Inf.* **2012**, *31*, 528–535. [CrossRef] [PubMed]
80. Abella, A.; Ortiz-de-Urbina-Criado, M.; De-Pablos-Heredero, C. The Process of Open Data Publication and Reuse. *J. Assoc. Inf. Sci. Tech.* **2019**, *70*, 296–300. [CrossRef]
81. Gassmann, O.; Enkel, E. Towards a Theory of Open Innovation: Three Core Process Archetypes. In Proceedings of the R&D Management Conference (RADMA), Lisbon, Portugal, 6–9 July 2004.

82. Nerone, M.A.; Canciglieri, O., Jr.; Steiner, M.T.A.; Young, R.I.M. Mapping the Open Innovation Ecosystem: An Analysis of the Technical and Strategic Level. In *Advanced Materials Research*; Han, J., Jiang, Z., Liu, X., Eds.; Trans Tech Publications Ltd.: Zurich, Switzerland, 2014; Volume 945–949, pp. 450–460. [CrossRef]
83. Dahlander, L.; Gann, D.M. How Open is Innovation? *Res. Policy* **2010**, *39*, 699–709. [CrossRef]
84. Villareal Larrinaga, O.; Landeta Rodríguez, J. El Estudio de Casos como Metodología de Investigación Científica en Dirección de Economía de la Empresa. Una Aplicación a la Internacionalización. *Investigaciones Europeas Dirección Economía Empresa* **2010**, *16*, 31–52. [CrossRef]
85. Wilkinson, M.D.; Dumontier, M.; Aalbersberg, I.J.; Appleton, G.; Axton, M.; Baak, A.; Blomberg, N.; Boiten, J.W.; da Silva Santos, L.B.; Bourne, P.E.; et al. The FAIR Guiding Principles for Scientific Data Management and Stewardship. *Sci. Data* **2016**, *3*. [CrossRef] [PubMed]
86. European Commission. Implementation Roadmap for the European Open Science Cloud. Commission Staff Working Document 2018. Available online: https://ec.europa.eu/research/openscience/pdf/swd_2018_83_f1_staff_working_paper_en.pdf (accessed on 11 March 2019).
87. Ortiz-de-Urbina-Criado, M.; Nájera-Sánchez, J.-J.; Mora-Valentín, E.-M. A Research Agenda on Open Innovation and Entrepreneurship: A Co-Word Analysis. *Adm. Sci.* **2018**, *8*, 34. [CrossRef]

© 2019 by the authors. Licensee MDPI, Basel, Switzerland. This article is an open access article distributed under the terms and conditions of the Creative Commons Attribution (CC BY) license (http://creativecommons.org/licenses/by/4.0/).

MDPI
St. Alban-Anlage 66
4052 Basel
Switzerland
Tel. +41 61 683 77 34
Fax +41 61 302 89 18
www.mdpi.com

Future Internet Editorial Office
E-mail: futureinternet@mdpi.com
www.mdpi.com/journal/futureinternet

www.ingramcontent.com/pod-product-compliance
Lightning Source LLC
LaVergne TN
LVHW070543100526
838202LV00012B/368